THEN AND THERE SERIES
GENERAL EDITOR
MARJORIE REEVES

Children at Work
1830–1885

ELIZABETH LONGMATE

Illustrated from contemporary sources

LONGMAN

LONGMAN GROUP UK LIMITED
Longman House,
Burnt Mill, Harlow, Essex CM20 2JE, England
and Associated Companies throughout the world.

First published 1981
Sixth impression 1987

Set in 11/12½pt Baskerville, Monophoto 169

Produced by Longman Group (FE) Ltd
Printed in Hong Kong

ISBN 0-582-22294-X

Contents

To the Reader

This book tells you about the work done by children in Britain between 1830 and 1885. Many of them worked very hard, as you will discover. You will probably think 'Why did they put up with it? I wouldn't.' But you would have put up with it too. If you and your family were in danger of either starving, or being separated from each other and sent to a workhouse, which was like a very grim prison, you would prefer to work. You would naturally want to help your family.

Throughout history of course, children have worked alongside their parents and learnt how to do adult jobs in that way. However, in the nineteenth century for the first time it became common for children to work in the new *factories* instead of at home with their parents. At the same time the population was increasing rapidly, families were very big, and it was difficult for some fathers to get work, even when there were jobs for the children.

Nowadays children are not allowed to go out to work, and have to go to school. In the nineteenth century many children never went to school at all, and those who did go normally attended for only a year or two. It was not until after 1870 that children had to go to school.

This book tells you about the jobs done by children from 1830 to 1885 and how Lord Shaftesbury and others tried to reduce their hours and improve conditions. There is a list of 'Things to do' on page 88. Sometimes you will find a word written like *this*. You will find the meaning of these words in the Glossary on page 91. Sometimes a simple word, that you think you know, has more than one meaning.

PART ONE: RICHARD OASTLER AND THE TEN HOURS' MOVEMENT

1 Richard Oastler

In September 1830 Richard Oastler, who was *steward* of a large *estate* at Fixby near Huddersfield in Yorkshire, visited his friend, John Wood, who owned a *worsted spinning mill* at Bradford.

Richard Oastler,
who led the campaign
to help factory children

During the evening Wood said he was surprised to find Oastler so keen on ending slavery in the West Indies (a popular cause at that time) but taking no notice of the 'cruelties daily practised in our mills on little children'. Oastler listened with growing astonishment and concern while Wood described how small

5

children worked from six in the morning until seven at night, with only one half hour break for lunch if they were lucky, in the woollen spinning mills which had sprung up in hundreds in that part of Yorkshire, the West Riding, since the beginning of the century. He told of weary children strapped by *overlookers* and falling into unguarded machines. Many employers were keen on helping West Indian slaves, building local chapels, or demanding parliamentary reform, but were blind to the evils in their own factories. The only excuse for them was that they were competing with each other and feared to go bankrupt. Even good employers like Wood were afraid that if they treated their workers any better they would be ruined and driven out of business. Wood, who had the largest worsted spinning business in England, employed over five hundred people, most of them women and children. He had tried to persuade neighbouring employers to agree to limit working hours to ten a day but they had refused. As Oastler was about to leave to ride home, in the early hours of the next morning. Wood called him to his room. The mill-owner had spent a sleepless night, reading his Bible by candlelight. He made Oastler promise to 'try to remove from our factory system the cruelties which are practised in our mills'. So seriously did Oastler regard this promise that he devoted the rest of his life to carrying it out.

HUDDERSFIELD IN 1830
In Huddersfield, where Oastler lived, there were a great many mills, most of them for spinning *wool*. We know that by 1838 there were three *cotton* mills, one hundred woollen mills and three *silk* mills in and around the town. They were large sturdy stone buildings several storeys high, some working on water power, others with steam engines and tall smoking *chimneys*. The raw dirty wool was fed into machines which cleaned and combed it, then eventually put into a machine, developed from James Hargreave's 'Spinning Jenny', which wound the woollen thread on to bobbins. Inside, the mills were very noisy, dirty, hot and in some work rooms very damp. Half the workers were under twenty-one, many of them small girls.

6

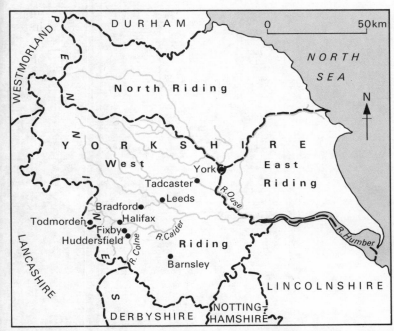

Yorkshire, showing Huddersfield and the woollen towns of the West Riding

Huddersfield was in the west of Yorkshire, one of a group of woollen manufacturing towns all quite close together—Halifax, Bradford and Leeds were among the largest. Further west, across the Pennine Hills, lay the cotton manufacturing towns of Lancashire. Huddersfield was one of the more attractive of all these towns since the surrounding hills were not so steep and windswept as some, and in the town itself a local builder, Joseph Kaye, had built good houses. By 1830 Huddersfield had wide main streets, many fine stone houses, and several elegant public buildings. In the view of Huddersfield on page 8 the River Colne is immediately in front of the town. The round building in the centre is the Cloth Hall, where handloom *weavers* sold their cloth; on the right is the Parish Church, with the market place very near to it on the left. In the far distance, behind the Cloth Hall, was the waterworks; on the extreme right was the

Huddersfield cottages in the 1880s. Joseph Hebergam probably lived in a house like one of these

gasworks, which supplied gas for street lighting. To the right of the Parish Church are some closely packed small houses on a street called North Gate, where in 1830 a teenage mill-worker, Joseph Hebergam lived. Joseph was later to meet Richard Oastler and to help him in his campaign to get shorter hours for factory children and adult workers—the Ten Hours' Movement.

We have no picture of the house where Joseph lived, but this picture shows a row of working-class cottages, photographed in Huddersfield in about 1880, which had been standing in Joseph's time. Most working-class houses had one room downstairs and one upstairs, with no kitchen or bathroom. Up to fifty houses would share one lavatory. Inside each house there was usually one table, a few chairs and stools, possibly a box to

Opposite: *A view of Huddersfield drawn in 1830*

put clothes in, and one or two beds. Some families slept six in a bed, three at one end, three at the other. For blankets and sheets they often only had sacking. Breakfast was porridge or bread and tea. Lunch was a hurried meal of boiled potatoes occasionally with bacon. At tea-time there was bread, butter and tea, at supper-time porridge again. They might have meat once a week, on Sunday. Bread, home-made, cost 4d. (2p) for a 2 lb (1 kg) loaf. Butter was 10d. (4p) a lb ($\frac{1}{2}$kg), tea 4s. (20p) a lb, milk 1$\frac{1}{2}$d. ($\frac{1}{2}$p) a pint, meat 7d. (3p) a lb, sugar 6d. (2$\frac{1}{2}$p) a lb, and the oatmeal for thirty-one helpings of porridge cost 1d. ($\frac{1}{2}$p). Rents were from 12d. (5p) to 3s. 6d. (17$\frac{1}{2}$p) a week. Some families paid 1d. ($\frac{1}{2}$p) a week for each child to a funeral society, something it was wise to do when half the children died before they became adults. Younger children might have a year or two at school at 3d. (1$\frac{1}{2}$p) a week.

Every street had at least one public house, open most of the day and night. There one could even see little boys as young as five call for their glass of ale and drink it with much cursing and swearing, at the end of a day's work. Drunken factory children were such a nuisance in some towns on Sundays that special constables had to be sworn in to patrol the streets. The only holidays for factory workers, apart from Sundays, were one day at Christmas and two half days (beginning at 2 p.m.) in May and October.

THE FAMOUS LETTER

Oastler returned to Huddersfield, on 29 September 1830, determined to help the factory children. That evening he wrote to a local paper, the 'Leeds Mercury', a letter which was to become one of the most famous of the nineteenth century. Entitled 'Slavery in Yorkshire' the letter began by praising the campaign to end slavery in the West Indies, then suggested that its supporters should have given at least some of their attention to 'scenes of misery, acts of oppression, and victims of slavery, even on the threshold of our homes'. 'Thousands of our fellow-creatures', he said, 'are this very moment existing in a state of slavery MORE HORRID than are the victims of that hellish system

Let truth speak out, appalling as the statements may appear. The fact is true. Thousands of our fellow-creatures and fellow-subjects, both male and female, the miserable inhabitants of a *Yorkshire town;* (Yorkshire now represented in Parliament by the giant of anti-slavery principles,) are this very moment existing in a state of Slavery *more horrid* than are the victims of that hellish system—" *Colonial Slavery.*" These innocent creatures drawl out unpitied their short but miserable existence, in a place famed for its profession of religious zeal, whose inhabitants are ever foremost in *professing* " Temperance" and " Reformation," and are striving to outrun their neighbours in Missionary exertions, and would fain send the Bible to the farthest corner of the globe—aye in the very place where the anti-slavery fever rages most furiously, her *apparent charity,* is not more admired on earth, than her *real cruelty* is abhorred in heaven. The very streets which receive the droppings of an " Anti-Slavery Society" are every morning wet by the tears of innocent victims at the accursed shrine of avarice, who are *compelled* (not by the cart-whip of the negro slave-driver) but by the dread of the equally appalling thong or strap of the overlooker, to hasten, half-dressed, *but not half-fed,* to those magazines of British Infantile Slavery— *the Worsted Mills in the town and neighbourhood of Bradford ! ! !*

A piece of Oastler's famous letter of 1830 which told people about children's work in factories

"COLONIAL SLAVERY".' He then described the ill-treatment of children in Yorkshire mills, and called for *Parliament* to make laws to protect them.

Many people spoke about Oastler's letter. Some employers protested that they would be ruined if hours were shortened, and that anyway long hours of work were good for children. Many people wrote to Oastler telling him of even worse conditions in other *textile* factories in Lancashire, Yorkshire and Scotland. In Oastler's own town, Huddersfield, hundreds of families were living on one meal a day, of potatoes, paid for by their children's wages of 2s. (10p) a week. The fathers were unemployed, and were afraid that if their children were forbidden to work, or made to work shorter hours, their families would starve. But most working men supported Oastler's letter, and a mass meeting at Huddersfield in November 1830 passed a vote of thanks to him for exposing those 'canting hypocrites who travel to the West Indies in search of slavery, forgetting that there is a more abominable and *degrading* system of slavery at home'. Forty Bradford employers, led by John Wood, asked for

11

a law to limit children's working hours to eleven a day. However, forty more Bradford employers at another meeting declared that everybody must work, and said 'we think twelve hours a day is little enough'.

Throughout Lancashire and Yorkshire working men began to form Short Time Committees to press for shorter hours. One of the first was at Huddersfield. They met every week at the Ship Inn. One Sunday, in June 1831, six of them walked up the hill from Huddersfield to Fixby Hall to see Oastler and ask him to become their leader. All Oastler knew of factory conditions had come from talking to employers like John Wood. This was the first time he had actually listened to working men talking about their conditions of work. He was surprised by their 'sensible manner', their 'intelligence and their *civility*'. But he could not see himself as their leader. In politics he was a *Tory* whereas they were *Radicals*. In religion he was Church of England, whereas they were members of *Nonconformist* chapels. His friends were all 'gentry' and he thought like a gentleman—for example he thoroughly disapproved of the suggestion that the vote should be given to more people—one of the other great arguments of the early 1830s. Nevertheless, the Huddersfield Short Time Committee persuaded Oastler that he was the man to lead them. They called this agreement to work together the Fixby Hall Compact, and Oastler began to go to all their weekly meetings, and collected more and more evidence of factory conditions. He became the main leader of all the Short Time Committees in northern England.

Huddersfield employers were also organising themselves. In August 1831 ten of them gave a petition to their *Whig* M.P., which he agreed with and presented to Parliament. These employers declared that children in factories had 'wholesome and comfortable employment' and Parliament should not pass laws about it. At the same time Oastler's friend, Michael Sadler, who was an M.P., was trying to get Parliament to pass a law

Opposite: *A painting of Fixby Hall, Huddersfield, where Richard Oastler worked as steward, in charge of a large estate*

which would limit the working day in textile factories to ten hours. But the 'Leeds Mercury', which had printed Oastler's letter on Yorkshire Slavery now turned against him and said a ten hour day was ridiculously short. This didn't really surprise Oastler as the 'Leeds Mercury' had always been a Whig paper and most factory employers supported the Whigs. After this Oastler's many letters on 'Yorkshire Slavery' were either published as pamphlets or printed in the 'Leeds Intelligencer' which was Tory.

In December 1831 Oastler discovered he could speak to large crowds. At a mass meeting of over one thousand people at Huddersfield on Boxing Day his towering figure, his rich deep voice, passionate manner and flow of words held his audience spellbound. He described how a seven-year-old girl had been beaten to death in a mill, and held up a heavy strap which had recently been used in Huddersfield for beating mill children. Many more public meetings followed. Oastler was by now giving so much of his time to the Ten Hours' Movement that his devoted wife, Mary, learnt to imitate his handwriting so that she could write many of the business letters which formed part of his work as steward of the Fixby estates. Oastler was also spending a great deal of money, about £2,000 a year, on the cause. Some of it was his own, some came from public subscriptions, but a large part came from his mill-owner friend, John Wood, who, in his lifetime, contributed £40,000.

THE YORK MEETING

At Easter 1832 Oastler's Short Time Committees organised a huge meeting at York which working men from many Yorkshire manufacturing towns attended. Oastler urged them to come: 'as in one loud, long, thundering Voice let Yorkshire and all England hear you swear OUR CHILDREN SHALL BE FREE!!' Three main processions were to march from Huddersfield, Halifax and Bradford north-eastwards to York. At 5 a.m. on Easter Monday morning, in the dark, thousands of men assembled in Huddersfield market place, waiting for groups from outlying villages to join them. As the clock struck six, amid cheers and shouting many home-made banners were raised, several bands played 'God save the King!', and the long column of men set out, Oastler at their head, to walk the forty-six miles (74 km) to York. On their journey they passed through the rolling Yorkshire dales, with their stunted trees and cold winds, tramping, on the first half of their journey, through many sturdy but grim industrial villages and towns built of dark grey Yorkshire stone. Some of the marchers wore *clogs*, and those who did not possess coats had thrown large woollen pieces over their shoulders instead. One group carried, throughout their journey, a banner you can still see at the Tolson Museum in Halifax. On one side it had the words:

> OASTLER is our Champion.
> The TEN Hours BILL
> And We are Determined to have it.

And the other:

> We hate tyranny
> and oppression.

The Huddersfield marchers were greeted at Leeds in the

afternoon by church bells ringing a welcome, for the vicar sympathised with their cause. The Leeds Short Time Committee provided bread, cheese and beer at the White Cloth Hall Yard for each man who could produce a food ticket, which had been issued to him by his own Short Time Committee before the march started. Then the weary marchers went to local warehouses for a short sleep, lying on straw. Rain began to fall heavily and after waiting in vain for it to stop, they set out at midnight to march the final twenty-two miles (35 km), Oastler still leading. A few torches were bobbing here and there in the column; throughout the stormy night the men sang old hymns and folk songs to keep up their spirits.

The next day 24,000 marchers gathered at the Castle Yard in York and listened patiently to their leaders—Oastler, John Wood, Michael Sadler M.P., Parson Bull and others— throughout a five-hour meeting. One unexpected speaker was the High Sheriff who congratulated them on their good conduct. On Tuesday evening they began the long march back through rain and wind, with a brief rest and scanty breakfast in some stables and barns at Tadcaster. The Huddersfield men did not arrive home until late on Wednesday evening. When Oastler took off his stockings that night, the skin of his feet peeled off with them.

Oastler's enemy, the 'Leeds Mercury', falsely reported that the marchers had been badly behaved and disorganised. In revenge the Leeds factory workers, after the public houses closed on the next Saturday evening, roamed their town in a hilarious mob, cheering the offices of newspapers which supported them, singing 'Rule Britannia' outside the houses of their own leaders, and finishing up outside the 'Leeds Mercury' office where they lit a great bonfire on which they burnt a figure of the editor, carrying a placard 'The great Liar of the North'.

Opposite: *An engraving of Castle Yard, York, where the 1832 meeting was held*

2 The 1832 Factories Report

Oastler had certainly drawn public attention to the plight of the factory children. His friend, Michael Sadler, the M.P., was now trying to persuade members of Parliament to pass a law which would mean that children could not work more than ten hours a day and forbid their employment for night work. Sadler reminded the members that they had recently ordered that West Indian slaves should not work between 6 p.m. and 6 a.m. Those who were against him said that British industry faced ruin, from foreign competition, if Parliament interfered with the employers' right to make their workers work as long hours as they pleased. They told Sadler it was sad but, 'the children must either work or starve'.

However, many members of Parliament did feel that they needed more information before they made a decision, so a Committee of thirty-seven M.P.s, with Michael Sadler as its chairman, met almost daily from April to August 1832 in London to find out about factory conditions. Altogether they heard evidence from eighty-seven people including sixty textile workers, twenty-one doctors and two clergy. Oastler and the Short Time Committees collected the *witnesses*. This was difficult as many feared that they would lose their job if they talked to the Committee, and in fact several were sacked. Sadler and Oastler worked long hours drawing up lists of suitable questions and helping the witnesses prepare what they wanted to say.

Opposite: *A typical industrial town—Sheffield in 1832*

One of the most interesting witnesses was Joseph Hebergam, a seventeen-year-old boy from Huddersfield. Joseph had met Oastler early in 1832 when he had asked Oastler for help. Joseph was crippled as a result of his factory work, and had to wear leg irons from the ankle to the thigh. He could not afford to have them lined with padding, so they were uncomfortable. When they heard his story Oastler and his friend John Wood immediately gave Joseph the money he needed, found him a place in Leeds *Infirmary*, and later arranged his journey to London where he gave evidence to the Committee. Joseph had begun work at the age of seven in a worsted spinning mill. Here are some quotations from what he said, taken from the Committee's Report. (The questions were asked by different members of the Committee. Every question and answer was numbered.)

4151. What were your hours of labour at that mill?
From five in the morning till eight at night.

4152. What intervals had you for refreshment and rest?
Thirty minutes at noon.

4155. What wages had you at that time?
Two shillings and sixpence a week [$12\frac{1}{2}$p].

4165. Was the main business of one of the overlookers that of strapping the children up to this excessive labour?
Yes, the same as strapping an old restive horse that has fallen down and will not get up.

4206. Is one part of the discipline of these mills profound [deep] silence?
Yes, they will not allow them to speak; if they chance to see two speaking, they are beaten with the strap.

4176. Where is your brother John working now?
He died three years ago.

4177. What age was he when he died?
Sixteen years and eight months.

Opposite: *Women and children working in a Lancashire cotton mill in 1843, where thread was being made from the raw cotton*

4179. Did his medical attendants state that the *spinal affection* was owing to his having been so over-laboured at the mill?

Yes.

4183. And did it at length begin to affect your limbs?

When I had worked about half a year, a weakness fell into my knees and ankles; it continued, and it has got worse and worse.

4184. Was that weakness attended with very great pain, and the sense of extreme fatigue [tiredness]?

Yes.

4187. How far do you live from the mill?

A good mile.

4188. Was it very painful for you to move?

Yes, in the morning I could scarcely walk, and my brother and sister used out of kindness to take me under each arm, and run with me to the mill, and my legs dragged on the ground in consequence of the pain; I could not walk.

4196. Your mother being a widow and having but little, could not afford to take you away?

No.

4197. Would the *parish* have relieved you if your mother had taken you away?

No, she has oftentimes been to them, but she was no better for it.

4219. Do you believe that there were frequent errors in the clock by which your labour was regulated?

Sometimes during the time I worked at that place, it was a quarter of an hour too soon in the meal-time; we had just done *fettling*, and we had but half got our dinners, and he put the clock forward to one, and he rang the bell, and we were obliged to run back to our work.

4224. Is there not considerable dust in that employment?

Yes.

4225. Does it not injure your food very much?

Yes, you cannot take the food out of your basket or handkerchief but what it is covered with dust directly.

4304. What proportion of the children in the factories in which you have worked can write?

I do not think there is above one in a hundred that can write.

4307. Have any cases of accidents in mills or factories been brought into the Infirmary since you were there?

Yes, last Tuesday but one there was a boy brought in about five or six o'clock in the evening from a mill; he had got catched with the *shaft*, and he had both his thighs broke, and from his knee to his hip the flesh was ripped up the same as if it had been cut by a knife, his head was bruised, his eyes were nearly torn out, and his arm broken. His sister, who ran to pull him off, got both her arms broke and her head bruised, and she is bruised all over her body. The boy died last Tuesday night but one, about eight o'clock; I do not know whether the girl is dead, but she was not expected to live.

4308. Did that accident occur in consequence of the shaft not being *sheathed*?

Yes.

4309. Do not you happen to know that the shafts of mills could be sheathed at comparatively very small expense?

Yes, all could be boxed off for a very little expense. In the mill I worked at last I do not think it would take above ten shillings [50p] to box them all off; and a man has had his two fingers cut off for want of its being done.

Four other witnesses came from Huddersfield—John Goodyear, who thought he was 'about' forty-four years old, John Hanson, Daniel Fraser and Oastler himself. John Hanson said he thought employers were making machines lower so that younger children might be employed. Daniel Fraser described how the factory children sometimes tried to sing a hymn but then the overlooker would 'strike the strap and smack it as if it were a cartwhip, to make them silent'. The Committee asked Daniel Fraser to find out more for them in different parts of the country. He returned three weeks later and told them of child factory workers in Essex, Suffolk, and Hertfordshire. They normally worked a twelve-hour day and some started at the early age of five. One boy, twelve-year-old Richard Love, had a wound on his face when Daniel saw him, as he had just been hit by the overlooker for accidentally wasting some materials. Another boy, James Naylor, earned two shillings (10p) a week, but once lost seven pence (3p) from his week's pay for being two hours late on one day. When his indignant mother went to see the overlooker he said that this was the rule. James could either accept the rule, or leave his job and starve. Daniel Fraser was also asked to bring a silk worker from Watford to give evidence before the Committee, but the man refused, saying he was unwell, although Daniel discovered he was going to work. The man was afraid that if he gave evidence he might lose his job.

3 The 1833 Factory Act

The Factories Report contained evidence only for the workers; there was no time for the employers to give their evidence because Parliament was mainly occupied in 1832 with the struggle for the Whig Party's First Reform *Act*, which gave the vote to more men. The Whigs returned to Parliament with a greater majority after the general election at the end of 1832. Several Tory M.P.s who had sympathised with factory reform, including Michael Sadler, lost their seats. Another M.P. had to be found who would speak for his Bill. Eventually Lord Ashley (better known by his later title, Lord Shaftesbury) was persuaded to take over the task of speaking in Parliament for the Ten Hours' Movement and for child workers as a whole, a task which was to occupy the rest of his long life.

Shaftesbury had been very unhappy as a child. His parents had neglected him and when he was only seven they sent him away to a boarding school where he was cruelly treated. His family was rich and aristocratic and connected, by marriage, with two Prime Ministers. He could certainly have been a minister and perhaps Prime Minister. Instead, he chose to spend his life on a cause which made him unpopular with his fellow M.P.s, who were all wealthy men elected by middle- and upper-class votes.

Parliament refused to accept Shaftesbury's Bill, but the members insisted on another enquiry, this time by men called *Parliamentary Commissioners* who travelled to the West Riding of Yorkshire and visited the main towns. They were pursued by indignant processions of factory workers and children who told

25

Lord Shaftesbury, who took over the campaign to help factory children from Richard Oastler, and introduced the Factory Acts in parliament

them to go home. Leaders of the Short Time Committees asked them to take their evidence from factory owners in public but they refused. In Leeds they were mobbed in their hotel by factory children, in Bradford another mob of children trapped them in a mill yard from which they were unable to escape until the factory bell summoned the children back to work. In Huddersfield they were met by similar demonstrations, and the factory children sang the 'Song of the Factory Children' at them:

> We will have the Ten Hours' Bill,
> That we will, that we will;
> Or the land shall ne'er be still,

A
SPEECH

DELIVERED BY

RICHARD OASTLER,

AT A MEETING HELD IN THE MANOR COURT-ROOM,

MANCHESTER,

On Wednesday Evening, April 27th, 1833,

TO CONSIDER OF THE PROPRIETY OF

PETITIONING THE LEGISLATURE

TO PASS THE

TEN HOURS FACTORIES'

REGULATION BILL,

WITHOUT WAITING FOR THE REPORT

OF THAT

'MOCKERY of INQUIRY,'

THE MILL-OWNERS COMMISSION.

'THEIR DEEDS ARE EVIL.'

HUDDERSFIELD:

PRINTED BY J. HOBSON, SWAN YARD.

Sold by J. Doherty, Withy Grove, Manchester, and all Booksellers.

—

1833.

The title page of a pamphlet containing a speech made by Richard Oastler, in Manchester in 1833, urging Parliament to pass a Ten Hours Factories' Act

> Ne'er be still, ne'er be still;
> Parliament say what they will,
> WE WILL HAVE THE TEN HOURS' BILL

One evening Oastler made a speech against the Commissioners at a large meeting in Huddersfield market place. Afterwards the crowd threw wax figures on to a bonfire.

THE FACTORY ACT OF 1833

The Commissioners refused to be frightened however, and made their report, and the Government then made their own law and passed the Factory Act in 1833. It applied to all textile factories except *lace* and silk. No child under nine was to work in them. Children aged nine to thirteen were to work nine hours a day, and have two hours' schooling each evening. Young people aged thirteen to eighteen were to work up to twelve hours a day. There were to be four Government inspectors—the first *factory inspectors*—who could go into textile factories, take information, and prosecute owners if they were breaking the law. This was very important as in the past owners had been able to break Factory Acts because there were no inspectors to prosecute them.

Oastler and his friends were not at all satisfied with the Act, because while it gave children in textile mills a shorter day than they had asked for, it left teenagers and adults with a long day. Now it was going to be much harder to convince the public that a strapping young man needed his work limited to ten hours. But the Act was a step in the right direction. In March 1835, for example, Joseph Schofield, a leading figure in Huddersfield's main Chapel, was found guilty of working a little girl thirteen hours a day in his factory with no meal breaks, and was fined £3. The details of that and many other Huddersfield cases can still be seen today in a large book in the British Museum. The Huddersfield *magistrates* were obviously on the same side as the factory owners, for on one occasion, in 1836, the book records that they found two owners guilty of working teenagers more

28   than twelve hours a day but 'case proved, which the magistrates

admitted, yet unaccountable to say, they imposed no fine'. Oastler became so furious at such magistrates that he advised factory workers to tell their children

> to ask their grandmothers for a few of their old knitting needles which I will instruct [teach] them how to apply to the *spindles* in a way which will teach these law-defying mill-owner magistrates to have respect even to 'Oastler's Law' as they have wrongly designated [named] the factory law.

Many of Oastler's friends and helpers, including John Wood and Lord Shaftesbury, were shocked by his support for violent methods, and refused to have anything more to do with him. Violence proved unnecessary in Huddersfield where, according to the records, a factory inspector, Leonard Horner, became a magistrate in 1837 and he made sure that the owners were fined and that the money was given to local schools.

One of the many ways in which inspectors kept a check on working hours was the 'Time-Book'. For example, in textile factories where children aged nine to thirteen worked, the overlookers had to fill in, for every child every day, a Time-Book with pages divided into columns like the one you see here.

TIME-BOOK, No. 2.

Required to be kept where Children between Nine and Thirteen Years of Age are employed, to show the Time each Child under Thirteen Years of Age has worked during the Day.

Date.	Name of Child.	Begins Work in the Morning.	Breakfast.		Dinner.		Tea.		Absence from other Causes.		Stops at Night.	Signature of Overlooker.
			Stops.	Begins Work.	Stops.	Begins Work.	Stops.	Begins Work.	Stops.	Begins Work.		

Several Huddersfield factory owners were fined for not seeing that Time-Books were kept.

4 The End of the Ten Hours' Movement

Oastler was a sick man, suffering from a nervous breakdown, when he heard that his employer, Squire Thornhill who owned the Fixby estate, had dismissed him because Oastler had been leading more riotous protests in Huddersfield, this time against the building of a workhouse. As Oastler left Fixby Hall for the last time, massed bands played the tune 'See the Conquering Hero Comes!' and a procession of 15,000 people walked with his coach into Huddersfield. Unfortunately one of their banners, insulted Squire Thornhill. This made him angry and he sued Oastler because he owed him money. This was possible because Oastler had always spent rather too generously his own money, and the Squire's, on the tenants and the estate. Oastler was put in the Fleet Debtors' Prison in London from 1840 to 1844. During those four years he had many visitors including Shaftesbury, who wrote in his diary:

> July 13th (1841). Called on Oastler today in the Fleet Prison...No man has finer talents or a warmer heart; his feelings are too powerful for control, and he has often been *outrageous* because he knew that his principles were just. The factory children, and all the *operatives* owe him an immense debt of gratitude.

Oastler was fairly comfortable; he rented furniture for his cell, his wife lived in lodgings nearby, and a constant stream of visitors and gifts came to his cell. Every week he published a small magazine called 'Fleet Papers' which sold well. His supporters collected money for him; for example in Huddersfield in 1841 they held an 'Oastler Festival' in the Philosophical Hall where over six hundred people had a high tea, concert and dance, making a profit of £23 for him. At this event they sang new words to the National Anthem:

> God save our Factory King
> Oastler the Brave, we sing;
> Long live our King.

(Oastler had first been called 'King Richard', by his enemies who were making fun of him, but his friends had proudly adopted the title.) Eventually his supporters managed to get Oastler released from prison, in 1844, but he was too weak to take much part in the last stages of the Ten Hours' Movement.

Shaftesbury continued to work in Parliament for the ten-hour working day, and to pursue factory-owners who broke the law. A further step forward came when the Tory Government passed the 1844 Factory Act, which reduced children's hours in textile factories to six and a half a day, although it said that children could start work as young as eight—lower than before. Young people of thirteen to eighteen were still to work a twelve-hour day, but women were now to work no longer than young people. All factory machinery was to be fenced in to prevent accidents. Unlike the 1833 Act the 1844 Factory Act also applied to factories where silk was made.

When Shaftesbury ceased for a while to be a Member of Parliament, his place was taken by John Fielden, a mill owner of Todmorden in Lancashire, who had introduced a ten-hour day in his own mill years earlier. Fielden nursed the 1847 Ten Hours' Act through Parliament. This ordered that no woman or young person aged thirteen to eighteen should work in a textile factory more than ten hours a day. (The Act did not apply to lace-making factories.) For a time, employers worked women and children in relays or shifts, keeping the men at work for as much as fifteen hours a day, but an Act of 1853 insisted that factory work, including meal breaks, must be done between 6 a.m. and 6 p.m. From this time on most textile factories did work a ten-hour day. The ruin which some employers had feared did not in fact overwhelm them. For the next half century the textile industry became more prosperous than ever.

31

PART TWO: LORD SHAFTESBURY AND THE COAL MINES

5 Children Who Worked in the Mines

While Oastler and his friends were campaigning for factory children, there were other children working in just as bad conditions in *coal-mines*. Only seven miles (11 km) north-west of Oastler's home, over a hill and across the valley of the River Calder, was the old town of Halifax, with its sooty, cramped houses built in narrow valleys and rising up the slopes of steep hills. Thomas Moorhouse worked at the Windy Bank *Pit* in Halifax. Thomas was an illegitimate child who had been *apprenticed* by the *Overseer of the Poor*, with his mother's agreement, to be a *hurrier* for a *collier*, filling and pushing trucks of coal for him.

An inquiry was held between 1840 and 1842 to find out what it was like for children who worked in the mines. Its findings were printed in the 1842 Mines Report. In 1840 Thomas described his life to the men holding the inquiry, called Sub-Commissioners:

I don't know how old I am; father is dead; I am a chance child; mother is dead also; I don't know how long she has been dead; 'tis better na three years; I began to hurry when I was nine years old for William Greenwood; I was apprenticed to him till I should be twenty-one...he was bound to find me in *victuals* and drink and clothes; I never had enough; he gave me some old clothes to wear, which he had bought at the rag-shop...he stuck a *pick* into me twice in my bottom...He used to hit me with the belt...and fling coals at me; he served me so bad that I left him, and went about to see if I could get a job; I used to sleep in the cabins upon the pit's bank, and in the old pits that I had

This drawing, from the 1842 Mines Report, shows a girl hurrier pulling a wagon of coal along a narrow tunnel

done working; I laid upon the *shale* all night; I used to get what I could to eat; I ate for a long time the candles that I found in the pits that the colliers left over night; I had nothing else to eat; the rest of the hurriers did not know where I was; when I got out in the morning, I looked about for work, and begged of the people a bit; I got to Bradford after a while, and had a job there for a month while a collier's lad was poorly; when he came back I was obliged to leave; I work now here for John Cawtherly; he took me into his house, and is serving me very well; I hurry for him now, and he finds me in victuals and drink.

In the six Halifax coal-mines in 1840 there were at least thirty children, and seventeen of them were between five and nine years old. There was even one three-year-old child taken every day into the mine by his father. The child spent his time either holding a candle or sleeping. He was too young to do much useful work but it is possible that in Halifax, as elsewhere, the colliers themselves operated a quota, limiting the amount of coal (and therefore money) each could get, in order to spread out the work fairly. Under a quota a small child would count as

33

one quarter so that his father could get one and a quarter times as much coal as a man working alone. Most Halifax citizens knew nothing of what it was like to work in the mines; a local lawyer and clergyman were horrified, on their first visit to a mine, standing at the foot of a dripping shaft hundreds of metres underground, to see a small black object crawling out of a tunnel, two feet ten inches high (85 cm). They discovered it was a little girl who regularly worked twelve hours a day or more in the mine. They were even more horrified at Mary Barrett, aged fourteen, who worked at Spencer and Illingsworth's mine. She told them:

> I work always without stockings, or shoes, or trousers; I wear nothing but my shift; I have to go up to the *headings* with the men; they are all naked there; I am got well used to that, and don't care now much about it; I was afraid at first, and did not like it.

Another girl, Margaret Gomley, who worked in a Halifax coal mine said:

> They flog us down in the pit, sometimes with their hands upon my bottom, which hurts me very much; Thomas Copeland flogs me more than once in a day, which makes me cry.

In the same coal-mine Harriet Craven, aged eleven, was found crying very bitterly by a Sub-Commissioner who had been sent from London to find out about child labour—

> She informed me her *getter* had been beating her very cruelly because she was then about to leave her work [five o'clock] before she had hurried sufficient for his purpose. Both herself and sister informed me that he was constantly in the habit of ill-treating them; the several marks upon their persons, which they showed me, were sufficient proofs of it.

Injuries were also caused by accidents. Within three years (1837–40) in Halifax coal-mines fifty people died in accidents, of whom thirty-four were under eighteen years old. For example David Pellett, who was being hauled up the shaft 'was drawn over the roller by his own uncle and grandfather...just at the moment when their attention was called to a passing funeral.'

Over the country as a whole, there were 349 deaths caused by accidents in coal-mines in 1838. This table from a parliamentary report shows how they were recorded at the time:

Cause of Death.	Under 13 years of age.	13 and not exceeding 18 years of age.	Above 18 years of age.
Fell down the shafts	13	16	31
Fell down the shaft from the rope breaking .	1	..	2
Fell out when ascending	..	..	3
Drawn over the pulley	3	..	3
Fall of stone out of a skip down the shaft .	1	..	3
Drowned in the mines	3	4	15
Fall of stones, coal, and rubbish in the mines .	14	14	69
Injuries in coal-pits, the nature of which is not specified	6	3	32
Crushed in coal-pits	..	1	1
Explosion of gas	13	18	49
Suffocated by choke-damp	..	2	6
Explosion of gunpowder	..	1	3
By tram-waggons	4	5	12
Total	58	62	229

Even the Sub-Commissioner, finding out about what it was like to work in the mines, worked in some danger. In some passages deep underground, he said:

> I have had to creep upon my hands and knees the whole distance, the height being barely twenty inches, and then have gone still lower upon my breast, and crawled like a turtle to get up to the headings. In others I have been more fortunately hurried on a flat board mounted upon four wheels, or in a *corve*, with my head hanging over the back, and legs over the front of it, in momentary anticipation [in danger every moment] of getting scalped by the roof.

The inquiry into child labour in mines throughout the country was made between 1840 and 1842. The main areas in which boys and girls were employed underground in coal-mines were Yorkshire (including Halifax), north Lancashire, east Scotland and south Wales. There were also a few children working in ironstone, tin, copper, lead and zinc mines. It was not possible to discover exactly how many children worked in coal-mines because employers did not fill in the *questionnaires* sent to them, and the Sub-Commissioners could not visit every mine in the country. However, they did find that in Yorkshire for every 1,000 adult men working in coal-mines there were twenty-two adult women, 352 boys and thirty-six girls between the ages of thirteen and eighteen, and 246 boys and forty-one girls aged less than thirteen. Usually the mine-owner paid the men—the colliers or 'holers'—for the coal they produced, and the colliers paid their own assistants, the hurriers or pushers, who helped to fill the tubs (also called skips, carriages, corves or dans) and pushed or pulled them to the foot of the shaft. Some colliers also employed fillers to fill the *trucks*, pitchers to keep the coal level in the truck as it was being filled, and slack-boys who would rake the coal dust into baskets and throw it into the gobbing, the space from which the large coal had been cut. The youngest children in the coal mine, the *trappers*, were employed by the mine-owner to open *ventilation doors* in the underground passages to allow trucks to pass through. The doors had to be kept shut most of the time to force air round various passages for ventilation. A Sub-Commissioner described the work of small trappers in Yorkshire:

The trappers sit in a little hole scooped out for them in the side of the gates behind each door, where they sit with a string in their hands attached to the door, and pull it open the moment they hear the corves at hand, and the moment it has passed they let the door fall too, which it does of its own weight. If anything impedes [stops] the shutting of the door they remove it, or, if unable to do so, run to the nearest man to get him to do it for them. They have nothing else to do; but, as their office must be performed from the repassing of the first to the passing of the last corve during the day, they are in the pit the whole time it is worked, frequently above [more than] twelve hours a day. They sit, moreover, in the dark, often with a damp floor to stand on, and exposed necessarily to drafts. It is a most painful thing to contemplate [think about] the dull dungeon-like life these little creatures are doomed to spend—a life, for the most part, passed in solitude, damp and darkness. They are allowed no light; but sometimes a good-natured collier will bestow [give] a little bit of candle on them as a treat...To be in the dark, in fact, seemed to be the great grievance with all of them. Occasionally they are so posted as to be near the shaft, where they can sometimes run and enliven themselves with a bird's eye peep at the daylight itself...When we consider the very trifling [small] cost at which these little creatures might be supplied with a light, as is the case in the Cumberland *collieries*, there are few things which more strongly indicate [show] the neglect of their comfort than the fact of their being kept in darkness—of all things the most wearisome to a young child.

The older children, hurriers, in Yorkshire had to push trucks which weighed 8 cwt (400 kg) full or 2 cwt (100 kg) empty. A day's work would be twenty trucks, which meant pushing a total distance of about three and a half miles (5.5 km). The hurrier sometimes had to help the collier to sieve the coal when he was filling the truck. The child held the sieve, weighing 20 lbs (9 kg) when full of coal, while the collier threw the coal into it. The drawings in this chapter come from the 1842 Mines Report, and show a girl hurrier with a chain pulling a wagon of coal, and a boy and girl being hauled up a narrow mine-shaft by a woman with a handle. All worked at Elland Colliery in Halifax.

Horses could not be used in most mine passages as they were too low. One Yorkshire assistant underground steward explained that 'The horses are not so handy as Christians, and we could not do with them.' Many mine-owners never went underground and did not realise how the hurriers were treated;   37

A drawing from the 1842 Mines Report showing a boy and girl being hauled up a narrow mine-shaft

however one agent, who ran a coal mine for a Yorkshire owner, said bluntly: 'If the men were to overwork the hurriers I could not interfere.' Even those hurriers who worked for their own fathers could not be sure they would be treated kindly. A Sub-Commissioner noticed that Elizabeth Eggley, aged fifteen, who worked for her father in a Yorkshire coal-mine, picked up a huge piece of coal weighing at least one hundred lbs (45 kg), and lifted it three and a half feet (1 m) into a truck while her father stood idly by.

Many children in the mines had started work at the age of six. One collier told how

> Some boys go down as early as six, which ought not to be allowed. I think children go down into the pit much too soon. I hope not to be compelled [made] to take my children under twelve years of age; but necessity compels some men against their inclination [what they want to do].

There were also some colliers who believed that women and girls should not work underground. 350 colliers held a meeting in the Courthouse, Barnsley, in Yorkshire, in 1840 to discuss child labour with the Sub-Commissioner who had come to find out about mines in their district. They all agreed 'That the employment of girls in pits is highly *injurious* to their morals, that it is not proper work for females, and that it is a *scandalous* practice.' Only five of the colliers disagreed. These 350 miners told the Sub-Commissioner that working hours in Yorkshire coal-mines were usually eleven a day, from five or six a.m. until between three and five p.m. They were only allowed between half an hour and an hour for lunch. This was sometimes a hastily gobbled meal of bread and cheese taken by the coal face.

Average wages for small children, the trappers, were six pence (2½p) a day. Hurriers might get five shillings (25p) a week, teenagers eight to twelve shillings (40p–60p). A young man in his twenties would earn one pound or more a week. Some Yorkshire employers, in Bradford and Leeds, listed the ages and wages of workers in their pits in 1840 in a table like this:

Children.	Number of Children.	Total Amount of Wages per Week.			Average per Week.	
		£.	s.	d.	s.	d.
From 5 to 6 years of age	1	0	2	6	2	6
„ 6 to 7 ditto	8	1	0	0	2	6
„ 7 to 8 ditto	30	4	0	6	2	8
„ 8 to 9 ditto	75	11	6	5	3	0
„ 9 to 10 ditto	123	21	6	0	3	5
„ 10 to 11 ditto	161	32	6	6	4	0
„ 11 to 12 ditto	160	36	16	2	4	7
„ 12 to 13 ditto	191	51	2	9	5	4
	749					
Cases for which the return of wages is omitted	9					
Total	758					

Young Persons.	Number.	Total Amount of Wages per Week.			Average per Week.	
		£.	s.	d.	s.	d.
From 13 to 14 years of age	223	71	3	0	6	4
„ 14 to 15 ditto	196	70	9	0	7	2
„ 15 to 16 ditto	196	76	19	0	7	10
„ 16 to 17 ditto	147	63	9	6	8	7
„ 17 to 18 ditto	141	72	5	3	10	3
	903					
Cases for which the return of wages is omitted	6					
Total	909					

Most witnesses agreed that colliers' families, compared with their neighbours, lived fairly comfortably and were well fed. For example in Yorkshire the Sub-Commissioner found that

The children as well as the adults, have bread and milk, or porridge, to their breakfast; huge lumps of bread, and often bits of cheese or bacon, or fat, to their luncheon in the pit; a

Opposite: *Colliers' cottages at Long Benton, Northumberland (Tyne and Wear). You can see the colliery in the background*

hot meal when they come home at five or six, and often porridge, or bread and milk, or tea for supper...The contrast is most striking between the broad *stalwart* frame of the swarthy collier, as he stalks home, all grime and muscle, and the *puny*, *pallid*, starveling little weaver, with his dirty-white apron and feminine look.

Although they were usually well fed, colliers' families were not well washed. One collier, when asked how often he washed, replied:

COLLIER : None of the *drawers* ever wash their bodies. I never wash my body; I let my shirt rub the dirt off, my shirt will show that; I wash my neck and ears and face, of course...my sisters never wash themselves...they wash their faces and necks and ears.

SUB-COMMISSIONER : When a collier is in full dress he has white stockings and low shoes, and very tall shirt-neck, very stiffly starched, and ruffles?

COLLIER : That is very true, Sir, but they never wash their bodies underneath; I know that, and their legs and bodies are as black as your hat.

In some areas the colliers' houses were also dirty, with broken windows whose gaps were stuffed with rags or paper, and with perhaps old sacking for bedding. However in Halifax the homes were normally well cared for, and in a Report on health in towns, in 1845, an inspector remarked that 'the people of Halifax use water more liberally for washing their windows and floors, and even in some instances their lanes and streets, than in any other town I visited'.

In and around Halifax the colliers and their children also seemed reasonably well dressed. Most children had two sets of clothes, one kept for Sunday School, unlike some other parts of the country where colliers' children wore rags. Girls often wore trousers, or 'breeches', underground, and sometimes nothing else. Some wore a loose dress called a shift. Girl hurriers sometimes wore a belt round the waist with a chain passing between their legs to the truck, which they pulled by crawling forward on their hands and knees. Some wore shoes, 'great big shoes *clinkered* and nailed'. Boy hurriers usually took off their jacket, waistcoat and shirt when they arrived at the coal-mine and put on a flannel donkin (an under jacket) on top of which they placed two pieces of leather which went over the shoulders and were joined at the back to a chain and hook which were attached to the wagon they pulled. A boy's outer jacket would be made of thick coarse woollen material, and the average Yorkshire pit-boy owned two suits and three shirts.

All the descriptions, in this chapter, of children who worked in the mines, come from the 1842 Mines Report. Its full title is 'Children's Employment Commission. First Report of the Commissioners. Mines. H.M.S.O. 1842.'

6 The 1842 Mines Act

Lord Shaftesbury persuaded the Government to set up the inquiry which led to the 1842 Mines Report, and the 1842 Mines Act which was passed afterwards. In his diary on 7 May 1842 he wrote:

> The Report of the Commissioners is out—a noble document. The Home Office in vain endeavoured [tried] to hold it back; it came by a most providential [well-timed] mistake into the hands of members...The disgust felt is very great, thank God; but will it be reduced to action when I call for a remedy? [That is, will anything be done?]

The following week he wrote: 'the feeling in my favour has become quite enthusiastic; the Press on all sides is working most vigorously'. Shaftesbury managed fairly easily to persuade the House of Commons to accept his suggestions for a new law. Many members listened with tears in their eyes to his descriptions of children's work in the mines.

But the House of Lords were much more hostile; it was a long time before he could find a lord to speak for his Bill. One Lord thought a practical education in collieries was better than a reading education though he did not say which sort of education he would choose for his own children! The Government did not give Shaftesbury any help when he tried to get M.P.s to support his Bill, but at least they did not stop him either. Finally in 1842 the Mines Act was passed. It said that women and girls and boys under ten years old could no longer work underground in mines, and that there were to be Government inspectors who

44

would see that the law was obeyed. The Act did not say anything about how many hours they were to work or make any rules for making the mines safer. The Lords would not allow any laws to be made about safety in mines until 1850.

At the time the Mines Act was passed, Shaftesbury remarked in his diary 'Whatever has been done, is but a millionth part of what there is to do.'

PART THREE: CHILDREN WHO WORKED ON FARMS

7 Living and working on the land

A FARMER'S BOY

Half way between the factories and mines of Yorkshire, and the gentle farm lands of Dorset, from which Lord Shaftesbury drew his income, was the village of Barford, seven miles (11 km) from

Joseph Arch,
the farmer's boy,
who tried to help farm-
workers by forming a trade union

Stratford-on-Avon, in the heart of England. Here, in 1826, Joseph Arch was born. Later, Joseph wrote a book about his life which gives us a picture of what it was like for children who worked on the land in farming.

Joseph's father was a *shepherd*, 'a plodding man', and his mother an energetic independent woman who quarrelled with the vicar's wife, when she tried to make all the village girls have their hair cut, and read to her family from the Bible and Shakespeare. Joseph learnt 'the three Rs' (reading, 'riting and 'rithmetic) at the village school where he began at the age of six and left before he was nine. His first job was scaring crows off the corn, working twelve hours a day, for wages of only four pence ($1\frac{1}{2}$p) per day. After a year he became a ploughboy for six pence ($2\frac{1}{2}$p) a day. He set off for his day's work, often before sunrise, in *smock*-frock and hobnailed boots, with a satchel which had in it his lunch of barley bread and occasionally an apple dumpling (this he could not resist eating long before lunch time). By the time he was twelve he was driving a pair of horses and ploughing, for at first eight pence ($3\frac{1}{2}$p) a day, later nine shillings (45p) a week. In his late teens he became 'Champion Hedgecutter of England', winning first prize in a hedgecutting competition, and after that he organised a *gang* of twenty men, arranging contracts to mow fields and cut hedges, from which he made quite a good living. But he always remembered his childhood struggles, and the 'underfed, overworked, uneducated men' who remained agricultural labourers. Finally, in middle age, he spent much time trying to start an agricultural labourers' union, hoping that he would be able to make life better for country workers.

SHAFTESBURY IN A DIFFICULTY

Lord Shaftesbury, who had already done so much to improve life for people in factories and mines, was angry when Joseph Arch, 'an *agitator*', tried to form a union, though he did allow local farm labourers to meet in a schoolroom on his estates, and paid for their lights.

Shaftesbury didn't like it if other people criticised the working and living conditions for farm labourers on his family's Dorset farms (at St Giles, Cranborne, Pentridge, Gussage, Horton, Woodlands, Chalbury, and Hinton Martell). Once, when his father still owned the farms, a popular writer, Miss Harriet 47

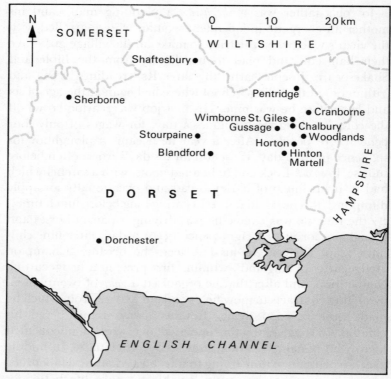

Dorset, showing Lord Shaftesbury's estates

Martineau, had accused him of championing factory children but taking no notice of the sufferings of farm workers especially the poorest in England, those of Dorset. 'He need but have gone into the *hovels* of his father's peasantry', she said, 'to have seen misery...which could not be matched in the worst retreats of the manufacturing population.' Shaftesbury could not persuade his father to pay better wages or repair cottages. His father said the money could not be found; so the embarrassed son made a passionate speech to local landlords and farmers begging them to treat farm workers better, even if his father would not.

A Government Report that same year (1843) quoted a Dorset farm labourer's wife:

A child bird scarer. This job was done by small children. They had to frighten the birds away by making a loud noise with a rattle

Rachel Hayward, Wife of John Hayward, Farm-labourer, Stourpaine, Dorset.

There are eleven of us in our family—myself, my husband, three daughters and six sons. We have two rooms,

Dorset Buttons. Little girls made these by hand with needle, thread and wire

one down stairs and the other up stairs over it. We all sleep in the bed-room. My husband gets 8s. [40p] or 7s. [35p] with a grist [corn], a bushel [36.5 litres], a week; my two eldest daughters get about 3s. 6d. [17½p] a week at buttoning, and three of my boys get 5s. [25p] a week together; in all about 16s. 6d. [82½p] a week. We have 16½ *lugs* of potato-ground, on which we grow potatoes and a few vegetables; for that we pay 7s. 7d. [38p] a year rent. We pay 1s. [5p] a week for the cottage, and coal and wood cost us 1s. 8d. [8½p] a week at this time of the year [December]. We get ¾ cwt [38 kg] of coal a week. I buy, besides, every week, ¾ lb [340 gm] soap, 1 oz [28 gm] tea, ½ lb [226 gm] bacon. I reckon we eat 1 lb [453 gm] of bread each a day; that, with potatoes, gives us enough. My three boys that are out at work went at nine years old.

The buttoning done by the girls was the making of buttons by filling in small wire rings with delicately patterned thread. The buttons were of various sizes—called mites, birdseye, jams, waistcoats, and outsizes—from about ¼ ″ (6 mm) upwards. The

girl would hold the wire ring in her left hand and closely cover it with buttonhole stitch, using a needle and linen thread. She smoothed the edge with a bone instrument called a slicker. She then built up the button on this foundation, again with needle and thread. Among the patterns the girls used were Old Dorset, Crosswheel, Honeycomb, Carolus, Yarrell, and High Tops. You can still see such hand-made buttons at the Dorset Museum in Dorchester. Button-making was done by many small Dorset girls until the mid-nineteenth century when a machine was invented to mass produce buttons. After that the little girls were set to work making gloves instead.

SHAFTESBURY'S IMPROVEMENTS

Despite Shaftesbury's speeches, Dorset children working in farming were still some of the poorest and worst-housed in England. When his father died in 1851 he became the owner of his father's farms. He wrote in his diary:

AUGUST 1851, ST GILES Inspected a few cottages—filthy, close, indecent, unwholesome. But what can I do?...the debts are endless...Every sixpence I expend—and spend I must on many things—is borrowed!...

OCTOBER 1851 Surely I am the most perplexed [worried] of men. I have passed my life in rating [criticising] others for allowing rotten houses and immoral unhealthy dwellings; and now I come into [own] an estate [where] there are things here to make one's flesh creep; and I have not a farthing to set them right.

By May 1853 he had decided:

...must sell old family pictures, must sell old family estates; it is painful; ancestral [family] feelings are very strong with me; but it is far better to have a well-inhabited well-cottaged property, people in decency and comfort, than well-hung walls which persons seldom see.

Shaftesbury had to spend much money on an expensive drainage scheme and on a law-case against a dishonest agent in charge of his Dorset lands. But he did manage to make great 51 improvements. An 1867 Report on the Employment of Children and Young Persons in Agriculture said approvingly of St Giles in Dorset, a village of 436 people, that the cottages 'belong to Lord Shaftesbury and are excellent. All have large gardens and allotments. Rent 1s. (5p). They have the opportunity of buying milk at a low rate'. At Cranborne the Report found that for Lord Shaftesbury's farm workers 'their hours of work were one hour shorter than usual, being from seven (having breakfasted first) till five all the year. Their rents were 1s. (5p) a week only.'

Shaftesbury had also employed scripture readers, restored churches, paid seven school mistresses and one curate, repaired and paid for some *almshouses* and made a rule that public houses on his land should close early.

AGRICULTURAL GANGS

Shaftesbury also saw that children were worked cruelly in other country areas, and he pressed for yet another parliamentary inquiry. The 1867 Children's Employment Commission on Agricultural Gangs found that many children, especially girls, worked as hard as factory children thirty years earlier. For example Mrs Anthony Adams, a labourer's wife of Denton in Huntingdonshire told them:

> In June 1862 my daughters Harriet and Sarah, aged...eleven and thirteen years, were engaged by a ganger to work on Mr Worman's land at Stilton. When they got there, he took them to near Peterborough; there they worked for six weeks, going and returning each day. The distance each way is eight miles [12¾ km], so that they had to walk sixteen miles each day on all the six working days of the week, besides working in the field from eight to five or half past five in the afternoon. They used to start from home at five in the morning, and seldom got back before nine. They worked at first on Mr Wyman's farm, close to the Peacock Inn, as you enter in for Peterborough, and afterwards they worked at Stanground. Sometimes they were put to *hoeing*, sometimes to *twitching*, and they had 7d.

*Mothers and children gleaning the fields
after the harvest*

[3p] a day. They had to find all their own meals, as well as
their own tools [such as hoes]. They [the girls] were good for
nothing at the end of the six weeks. They were very quick to
work, and the ganger never gave them the stick.

I never heard of his treating them with any impropriety.
It was a mixed gang, but the boys were not very big. The 53

ganger made a great fuss to have my children, because they were so quick in the work, and he persuaded me to send my little girl Susan, who was then six years of age. She walked all the way to Peterborough to her work, and worked from eight to half past five and received 4d. [2p]. She was that tired that her sisters had to carry her the best part of the way home—eight miles, and she was ill from it for three weeks, and never went again.

There were many such children working in farm gangs, especially in eastern England. They moved from farm to farm and were employed by the gang leader who then made arrangements with the farmer. In 1865 the vicar of Binbrooke in Lincolnshire, which had a population of 1,335 people, counted the number of people working in farm gangs in his parish. The details were recorded in the 1867 Report:

Ages	Male	Female
Under seven	0	0
Between seven and thirteen	39	42
Between thirteen and eighteen	3	34
Over eighteen	10	85

These gangs worked at distances of from half a mile (800 m) to five miles (8 km). Their hours, including time spent travelling, were 7 a.m. to 5.15 p.m. at the earliest, 6.30 p.m. at the latest. They were allowed a quarter of an hour for breakfast at 10 a.m. and one hour for lunch at noon. The vicar was distressed at the bad language, immoral behaviour, hasty marriages, and lack of education, which the gang system encouraged.

Many parents didn't want their children to work in farm gangs, but if the family was poor they had to let them go. Very poor families in a parish might be given a small amount of money by the Local Poor Law Board of Guardians. This money was called poor relief. In Spalding, in Lincolnshire, the Board said it did not give relief to 'boys of ten years of age, nor girls over eleven, in some cases twelve years of age, on the ground that they can get 6d. ($2\frac{1}{2}$p) to 9d. ($3\frac{1}{2}$p) a day at field work.'

School was something to be fitted in when there was no farm work to do. The mistress of a girls' charity school at the village of March in Cambridgeshire said in her evidence for the 1867 Report:

> The number of girls attending school in the winter is about 140. At the end of February or the beginning of March the girls begin to leave for field work. At the present time (May) we have only 45 out of the whole number. These children will probably not go out at all until harvest. They are either children who are too small to go to work, or children of a better class. Children leave this school for field work at eight years old. There are no infants in this school; they are only admitted at seven years of age. The children who have gone will not come back until after the potato picking is over; that will be about the beginning of November. Most of these children go to Sunday school, either at the Church or at some chapel. When they come back I find them very rough.... I very seldom hear any bad language from them while at school, but I know that their language is very bad when they are returning from their work, in the roads.

In Lord Shaftesbury's county, Dorset, where the farm workers were among the poorest in England, people wanted education, because they hoped to escape from farm work and poverty. Another Government Report, the 1867–78 Royal Commission on Women and Children in Agriculture, said there were an unusually large number of night schools in the villages in Dorset. It added that the farmers did not like the schools:

> Farmers in that country are especially suspicious of education, because it is found in practice that the low wages drive away almost all the young men who are sufficiently well educated to go.

55

Lord Sidney Osborne told the Commissioners that there had been a night school in his parish of Durweston for twenty-four years, and he thought that probably 129 children during that time had left the parish and 24 had left the country, as well as four families.

One of the Assistant Commissioners who had collected evidence for the Report in Dorset, Mr Stanhope, met the Blandford Board of Guardians (who were responsible for collecting the poor rate from householders and deciding who should be given poor relief) in October 1868. One of them, probably a farmer, told him: 'The less education labourers have the better. Whenever a boy can earn 2s. [10p] he ought to go to work. Some of my best men are uneducated. There is a school in my parish to which I do not subscribe.' (He meant that he gave no money to it.) The others applauded and there was a lively discussion during which everyone agreed that education for children had a bad effect on farm work and that children should not have to go to school, nor should the farmers pay any money for the schools. But Mr Stanhope then had a long discussion with the Board of Guardians, and eventually he persuaded them to agree, rather vaguely, that they were in favour of education. Before long they were not to have much choice, as in 1870 Parliament ordered that children must go to school and new School Boards were set up everywhere to collect school rates and build 'Board Schools'.

ONE DORSET FAMILY

While he was in Dorset, during 1868, Mr Stanhope also met a shepherd's wife who lived near Blandford. Her husband was better paid than farm workers. He earned 'ten shillings (50p) a week and the house, because he works on Sundays. He has £1 at harvest, and £2 at lambing.' She told him that she had

had twelve children that lived. There are seven living at

Opposite: *A photograph of some Dorset cottages, in Bradford Peverell in 1883. The children look as though they have been dressed in their best clothes to have their photograph taken*

home with me now. Our third bedroom was put up the summer before last. Before that time, we had only two, and we used all of us to sleep in them; at one time there were thirteen or fourteen of us. One of them is a tidyish room; in the other the door only opened for you to go in sideways. Downstairs we have only one room with a fireplace and we have to dry all the wet clothes, and sit there too.

She described her children's work:

We have three girls at home, the two eldest do a little gloving. I used to try to earn a good bit at buttoning when we were first married, but the gloving is not so good; if they come to sit at it all day, they might perhaps earn 1s. 3d. [6p] a week. My second boy was only seven when he went out to work. He was bird-keeping. He had 1s. [5p] or 1s. 6d. [7½p] a week. When a boy goes out he most times leaves school altogether. Now and then he goes back in the winter, but they don't generally allow it in the school.

Her boys, she said,

were put to go with the sheep between ten and eleven years old. They'd first get 2s. [10p], and 3d. [1½p] more for working on Sundays. They don't get their full pay till they get to be nineteen. There's our Jim, he's nineteen, and he gets 8s. 6d. [42½p] a week; next time he'll be raised, and will get 9s. [45p]. They all have to buy their own tools. I have known our boys lay out 9s. [45p] in tools.

Like everyone else they ate the same food all the time:

We live on potatoes, bread and pig-meat; we often sit down to dry bread. For harvest dinner we send out some boiled

Opposite: *This drawing shows the scene inside a Dorset farmworker's cottage in 1848. How many people can you see in the one room?*

potatoes, a bit of cabbage, and we put a bit of fat to the potatoes. We never have a bit of milk. They are very fond of butter. We drink tea; we give 6d. [2½p] and 8d. [3½p] for a quarter of a pound [113 gm] of tea.

The family also ate cheese. Some items were expensive, and it was a struggle to provide them:

Shoes are very dear; our little children's are 7s. [35p] or 8s. [40p], a man's 12s. 6d. [62½p]; one of my boys doesn't wear out above one pair in a year, but they must be proper good ones. We buy our firewood. Sometimes our wood will come to £2 for the winter. We have one blanket that was given to us. We had one that we got from a man who came round; we paid for it by 1s. [5p] a fortnight, we can't get enough money at a time to buy one.

But candles were cheap: 'We get our candles at 6d. (2½p) a lb (453 gm). In the winter that would last a week, they have to get up by candle light.'

SMALL BOYS IN DORSET

Mr Stanhope discovered that boys began farm work at an earlier age in Dorset than elsewhere, and worked longer hours. In his 1868–69 report, he described boys who followed the horses and plough:

The hours are very long (often from 5 a.m. to 7 p.m.); it gives little leisure to a boy, and requires him to walk every day at least ten or twelve miles (16–19 km) over ploughed ground. In most counties no farmer would think of putting a boy to such work, unless very exceptionally strong, before ten or eleven years of age; yet in Dorset many boys begin at seven or eight.

8 The Farmers

It is perhaps difficult for people nowadays to understand the farmers who paid such low wages and employed very young children. Most farm land was owned by landowners, like Lord Shaftesbury, and rented from them by farmers. During the first sixty-five years of the nineteenth century, after *enclosures*, the number of people who owned farms was less while the number seeking work as farm workers was very much greater. Families were large, and parents encouraged their children to work. There were farmers who felt they had a duty to provide work for any who needed it, but they did not feel that they should also pay generous wages. Also, in the mid-nineteenth century, as we can find out by reading local newspapers of the time (for example the 'Dorset County Chronicle') the farmers were very worried by the fall in the price of corn, following Sir Robert Peel's repeal of the Corn Laws in 1846. (You can read about this in another Then and There book called 'Robert Peel, Free Trade and the Corn Laws'.) They were bitterly upset that a fellow Tory had allowed foreign corn, from America and elsewhere, to enter the country freely and, as years went by, in increasing amounts. They were afraid they were going to be ruined by cheap foreign corn, and also, a little later, by refrigerated meat coming from Australia and New Zealand. However, as well as these real fears, the farmers also had firmly fixed in their minds the idea that it was quite right that they should have a more comfortable life than their farm workers. They would pay £42 for a horse to be used for a carriage or hunting, £27 a year for a child's schooling, or £3 10s. (£3.50) for a gun, and yet they expected a large labourer's family to live on 9s. (45p) a week. Later, looking back, farmers saw the years 1850 to 1875 as a Golden Age for themselves, if not for their farm workers, and the years 1875 to 1900 as a time of depression for farmers, although by then the farm workers' wages were rising.

Farm labourers' wages did not get better until the late nineteenth century when many country people had moved to the towns or even left Britain altogether to go and live in Canada, Australia or New Zealand. Year after year local papers carried such advertisements as this one in the 'Dorset Country Chronicle' in January 1851, and many people, especially young men and women, must have been tempted by them to seek a better life:

> For Adelaide and Port Phillip. To sail early in February, the magnificent Frigate-built Indiaman 'City of Manchester' 1,800 Tons, to Load at the Jetty, London Docks. This splendid vessel has ten feet [3 m] in height between Decks, and offers unrivalled accommodation to Cabin and intermediate Steerage Passengers. Intermediate Passage £15. She will call at Plymouth and carry an experienced surgeon.

9 Laws about Children who worked on the land

For those who stayed in Britain, life gradually got better, partly because of changes in the law. Following the Report of the Commission on Agricultural Gangs (described on page 52) the 1868 Gangs Act forbade the employment of children under eight in gangs, and said that women and girls could only work in gangs when accompanied by a licensed gang-mistress. The master of a gang had to be licensed by local J.P.s, who must make sure that he was fit for the position. Fortunately this Act of Parliament really did something for people, and the worst evils of gang labour disappeared, although it was still very hard work.

Then the 1873 Agricultural Children Act for England and Wales said that no child under eight was to be employed in any form of agriculture except by his parents. Children aged eight to twelve, if they wanted farm work, had to produce a certificate from their teacher to show that (if they were under ten) they had completed 250 school attendances in the last year, or (if aged ten to twelve) 150 attendances. But local courts could allow these rules to be broken for up to eight weeks a year. Exceptions were also allowed during harvesting, where the school was more than two miles (3.5 km) from the child's home, or where a school inspector certified the child had reached the fourth standard. At first this Act was not always obeyed, and some farmers did not bother to ask for a child's certificate of school attendance. However, by 1880, education had become compulsory for every child throughout the country, by 1899 the official leaving age was twelve, and as time went on inspectors checked up to find out if any children were playing truant or employers were breaking the rules.

Children went on working on farms for a long time, and farm labourers' families have always had a struggle to make ends meet. Nevertheless the story sometimes ended happily. In October 1885, when Lord Shaftesbury died, the 'Dorset County Chronicle' wrote about the farm labourers' cottages in his own village:

> The village of Wimborne St Giles, near his family seat [house] of St Giles, was transformed under his care into a model little village. He built new labourers' cottages, each containing a front parlour and kitchen on the ground floor, with three bedrooms above, absolutely unconnected with each other. Every cottage has its apricot tree, its pump, its sanitary arrangements, its pigsty, its quarter-acre allotment. Almshouses and other advantages are offered to those who are beyond work. Amid all other engagements he never forgot that *charity* which begins at home.

PART FOUR: OTHER CHILDREN'S WORK

10 Reports on Children's Employment in the 1860s

STAFFORDSHIRE POTTERIES

Despite the leadership of Lord Shaftesbury and others, changes were often slow to come. For example, in June 1862, a Doctor J. B. Davis of Shelton in Staffordshire wrote despairingly to the Commissioners who were enquiring about child labour in the Potteries, pointing out that he had supplied the same evidence twenty-one years earlier and yet 'there has been little change during the last twenty years'. Nevertheless he took the trouble to describe children's work in the Potteries again. The platemakers' *mould runners* were, he said, little boys who

> have to take the mould from the platemaker, when charged with the newly moulded clay plate, and carry it into a very hot stove to dry. These boys are very thinly clad, they generally have a pair of trousers and a shirt on, and are without shoes and stockings, and are kept on the run all day long. They carry from thirty to fifty dozens [360–600] of these charged moulds into the stove, besides stopping there to take the dried plates off the mould to be refilled. The boys here carry two moulds at once. An attempt has lately been made to relieve them from the great heat of the stove by having ventilators placed at the top and the bottom of each stove. But these ventilators lower the heat of the stove, and thus prevent the rapid drying of the plates, hence it often happens in *manufactories* in which the ventilators have been introduced they are closed by the platemakers.

> The platemaker has another boy called a *jiggerer*, who stands and turns the wheel or jigger on which the

platemaker works all day long. Those who make saucers and bowls also have a jiggerer. In this way the platemaker has two boys in attendance upon him, the mould runner being required in addition to wedge the clay, a very laborious occupation.

I fear the boys generally are somewhat abused. In many manufactories the workmen are allowed to hire, to pay, and to discharge these boys, quite independently of the manufacturer. In this way the boys are got for these laborious duties as cheaply as possible, and, where his master is not strictly honest or is addicted to intemperance [he means 'drink'] the boy sometimes loses a portion or even the whole of his wages. In these and similar cases I have often noticed these thinly clad and ragged lads going about the town to beg bread during the meal hours when they were regularly at work.

The age of the mould runners is from eight to twelve years, none of them being above twelve.

There is a series of oven boys, from about ten to twelve years of age, who are employed to get in and prepare the coals inside the hovels, to be put into the ovens for the purpose of firing the ware. Each oven requires about five tons of coal. These young boys are required after their day's work to sit up with the fireman all night to attend to the ovens. This may happen about twice a week.

It may be asked what is the future career of mould makers who survive... They frequently become platemakers in their turn. It is a rare thing to meet with a platemaker beyond forty-five years of age.

Although the boys' lives had not changed in twenty years, the M.P.s, employers and people generally were now shocked to think children worked like this. It was thanks to Shaftesbury that they had changed their minds. Some potteries employers

Opposite: *Children carrying clay in brick yards in 1871. Similar work was done by children in the potteries*

actually suggested to the Assistant Commissioner collecting evidence about child labour that no child under ten should be allowed to work in the potteries, and that older children's hours should be reduced.

SEWING TRADES

The work done by small girls making lace or gloves might seem easier, but the hours were long and the work was boring. Girls as young as seven were sent by their mothers to a 'lace school' run by a 'schoolmistress' who paid them nothing for their work for the first year, and might charge a few pence a week if she taught reading and writing as well as lace making. Once a girl could make herself useful, she would earn between 1s. (5p) and 2s. 6d. ($12\frac{1}{2}$p) a week, working from 8 a.m. to 5.30 p.m. each day. Sarah Kingham, aged twelve, who gave evidence to a Commissioner for the 1863 Children's Employment Commission Report, worked for a Mrs Burnidge in Houghton Conquest, Bedfordshire. The work room was about $11\frac{1}{2}$ feet (3.5 m) square, the size of a small living room nowadays, and contained twenty-four girls, a mistress, and two other people. Sarah had learnt to read but not write. She could read the word 'remember' but did not know what it meant (when asked if it was different from 'forget' she said she did not know). She had not heard of France, but had heard of people going to Australia in a ship. She did not know what the 'sea' was. She did however go to Sunday school. Girls working in such places sometimes caught tuberculosis, an unpleasant and in those days fatal lung disease, or they had trouble with their eyes in the crowded stuffy candle-lit rooms.

Gloves were still knitted on hand frames in the 1860s, although they could be made faster on modern machines in factories. The work was done by families. Mary Thorpe, a young woman of Bulwell village near Nottingham, described the struggles of her family and friends to make a living from this old-fashioned craft. The men made the knitted pieces for the gloves, which were then stitched together by children, who had to work very long hours at the end of each week because:

68

the men are 'shacking' [taking time off] at the beginning. On 'Saint Monday' they will go pigeoning or on some other amusement, and do little on Tuesday beyond setting the winders [little boys who wind skeins onto bobbins] to work, and most do not begin regularly till Wednesday. The work is always behind, and comes in to the stitchers at all times on Friday night, up to twelve, and one, and two. They must sit up to do the work then as the gloves have to be finished and taken into Nottingham in the morning. Children younger than seven are kept up till eleven and twelve. Mothers will pin them to their knee to keep them to their work, and if they are sleepy give them a slap on the head to keep them awake. If the children are pinned up so, they cannot fall when they are slapped, or if they go to sleep. The child has so many fingers set for it to stitch before it goes to bed and must do them. My little sister, now five and a half years old, can stitch a good many little fingers, and is very clever, having been at it for two years. She used to stand on a stool so as to be able to see up to the candle on the table. Boys stitch fingers too sometimes. I have seen a boy twelve years old, come home from winding at 8 or 9 p.m., and then set to stitch three dozen fingers, that is the fingers of thirty-six pairs of coarse gloves. I have heard him ask 'Am I big enough to be a sailor?'

Another girl in Bulwell, Elizabeth White, aged eleven, worked long hours in a neat but very poor home, with her mother and five-year-old sister, Jane. The Commissioner collecting evidence found that 'this child looked cheerful and well, though I was told that the family are sometimes a day almost entirely without food'.

Some children worked on the preparation of straw plaits, used for making bonnets. Their parents would send them to a plait mistress when they were very small, partly to be cared for all day and partly to learn the skill of plait making. Some plait mistresses said they taught the children to read and write as well. Mrs Ann Tompkins of Houghton Regis in Bedfordshire ran a 'Straw Plait and Infant School' in the mid-1860s. The Commissioner reported:

> In this cottage I found forty infants and their mistress in a room 11'2" × 10'8" × 7' 9" high [that was very small]. The window was open, it being summer, but still the air was offensive [unpleasant]. The infants ranged from between one and two up to about six or seven years old. The younger were merely being taken care of, the elder employed on straw plait, and two or three on sewing. I saw the children at work, and the little clippers had their scissors tied to their waists. The mistress had beside her a stick full a yard long, which on my entry she put out of sight, but she was too old to seem able to hurt them seriously with it.

The mistress told him:

> The children come here from about 9.30 a.m. till 12.30 a.m., and from 2 p.m. till 5 p.m., but some parents can't keep them so much as an hour at home at dinner time. I like to have 3d. [1p] a week, for which I take care of them and teach a little reading. Children are taught plaiting usually at four years old, some at three and a half, and they can clip the loose straws off younger, when about three and a half or three. Lizzie Ibbins there, who is between two and three years old, is clipping some plait made by her sister...Lizzie Cook, who was three last month I think, can clip her 'ten' [yards] in the day, which Lizzie Ibbins has never done yet. George Tompkins, aged three and a half, a relation of ours, is the youngest plaiter here, but he can only do a yard or two in the day.

The Commissioner then talked to Mary and Jane aged four, Sarah aged three, and Alfred aged five, who gathered round and told him solemnly about their work. Later he discovered that older children earned 3s. (15p) or 4s. (20p) a week. Adults could make between 7s. (35p) and 9s. (45p) a week from plaiting. As the farm labourer's wage, in that area, had recently fallen from 10s. (50p) or 11s. (55p) a week to 9s. (45p), we can see why very poor parents should try to train their children for such work.

There were some children who appeared to enjoy their work, and take a pride in it, despite long hours. For example, Elizabeth Ann Hammel aged twelve, who worked for Mrs Rogers, a wholesale milliner (hat and cap maker) of Rochdale Road, Manchester, said in 1864 that she began when:

> I was not quite eleven. My hours and meals are from 9 a.m. to 8 p.m., with an hour for dinner and half an hour for tea. Have stayed till 9 or 10 p.m. perhaps twice a week, but never later than ten minutes or so past 10 p.m., and that very seldom. Sometimes take only a quarter of an hour for dinner; but I live a quarter of an hour off, so that I must be away towards an hour. Now I am out of my apprenticeship I earn 4s. (20p) a week here at making caps. The room is too small for us to have a fire, and we did not even in the frost lately, but we have gas lighted all day instead. It is very comfortable—always warm.

MATCH MAKING

A small number of children made matches which was very unhealthy work. Bundles of matches had to be dipped in a mixture of *phosphorus* and glue, shaken, and then rolled to separate the matches. Mr J. E. White, the Commissioner who had investigated glove making, also discovered many details about match manufacture in the same year, 1863, in London. He reported that phosphorus caused 'necrosis of the jaw', known to the children as 'the flute' or 'the compo': 'The disease begins with toothache. This gradually becomes more violent and more constant, the gums and face swell, and the teeth decay and fall out.' Later, parts of the jaw bone dropped off, and, as one doctor told Mr White, 'after lingering for a longer time than you would think possible, he is at last worn out and dies.'

At John Baker's match factory in Bethnal Green the match making was done by two boys

in one low narrow loft, with hardly any ventilation but the door. On each side of the stove, which is at one end, far from the door, are two small drying rooms with open doorways into the loft. Close to this end was one boy dipping bundle dips, the other working close by him shaking out the bundles. Large quantities of matches are stored in the middle of the loft. The air, especially near where the boys work, feels loaded with phosphorus. In a separate building a girl works at stamping wood shavings into proper lengths for making boxes. Charles John Garner, age 14, has been here three years. Dips, boxes, does everything. Comes in the morning at 7, stays till 6. When they are busy, stays at work till 10 or 11. He does not go home [until] then to sleep. Is allowed one hour for dinner, half an hour the two other times [breakfast and tea]. Washes and changes his waistcoat before going home. Could not go in this because it smells so. Has lost his voice rather. 'I don't seem to speak so much'. Has got a cough. Has lost two or three teeth. The others ache sometimes. Takes his wages home to mother. Makes generally 4s. 7d. [23p] or 5s. [25p] a week. Can read a little.

Charles's younger brother, John, aged twelve, who worked with him, remarked that he could 'see his brother's clothes as well as his own shine very much at night' (the effect of the phosphorus). He also had aching teeth. John remarked rather pathetically 'Mr Rogers took my name once. That was for a holiday. Mr Rogers was a very nice gentleman.' Perhaps he was hoping that the Commissioner had some holidays to offer too.

CLIMBING BOYS

It took a hundred years from the time when people first protested about the use of small boys to climb up the inside of

Opposite: *Children and grown-ups making matchboxes at home for Bryant and May's factory in the East End of London in 1871*

chimneys and sweep them, until this was finally stopped. Again it was Lord Shaftesbury, who finally brought success.

Climbing boys were often illegitimate children who were sold, at the age of five or six, by their mothers to chimney *sweeps*. Their skin was hardened by rubbing in salty water, but for the first year their elbows and knees would be raw. The chimneys they had to climb might be only twelve inches square (300 mm), and their masters encouraged them by lighting fires beneath them, or by pricking their feet with pins. When he reached the top of the chimney the boy climbed slowly down again, sweeping the thick layer of soft black sticky soot as he went. Climbing boys were always black, as they never washed, and they slept beneath the sack in which soot had been carried. They were likely to get a particularly unpleasant form of cancer. When coal began to be used a great deal in the eighteenth century, more climbing boys were used. In 1773 a man named Jonas Hanway began to protest about their suffering. Then Lord Shaftesbury fought for them, and on several occasions, from 1840 onwards, persuaded a reluctant Parliament to make laws forbidding the employment of climbing boys. Although he managed to make people feel sorry for climbing boys, they did not feel sorry enough to stop employing them; they were afraid that if they allowed sweeps to use machines instead of boys, a little soot would fall on their carpets and furniture. Also, in some houses a builder might have to be paid to make the chimneys bigger and more convenient for using machines. Many sweeps became disgusted at the cruelty they admitted they had to use on their boys, but they found householders insisted on having them. Several master sweeps became leading supporters of Shaftesbury's 'Climbing Boys' Society', which collected information about climbing boys, prosecuted cruel masters, and spread news about the worst cases.

One such master sweep was Mr Peter Hall of Wellington Road, Stockport, who gave evidence in 1863 about the ways in which the 1840 Act was being broken. He said:

I have been requested, as agent for the North Staffordshire

and Birmingham Association for Preventing the Employment of Climbing Boys, to tender [give] my evidence to the Children's Employment Commissioners. I am now fifty-eight years of age. I was brought up as a climbing boy from the age of six and a half, apprenticed to one of the best masters in the trade. I have taken an active interest in the subject for the last twenty years, and have been instrumental in obtaining at least four hundred convictions. [he meant that he had helped to bring 400 cases to court] The [1840] Act is defective [not good enough]. It is violated [broken] to a great extent, and this illegal practice is very much on the increase. In Sheffield there are twenty-two, varying from five to ten years of age. There are fourteen at Chester. At Nottingham there are twenty.

One that knows the trade, as I do, can always tell what they are going to do with the child from the look of them, but they [the sweeps] say they have him to carry the things; but the doors are all locked, and the blinds pulled down, and the windows fastened, as soon as they get into a room; so that it is not easy to catch them.

The magistrates are very often dead against us; I had seven cases in one town, in none of which they would convict; so are the police frequently [against them]. In one case the defendant had absconded [run away], the police would not take the trouble to look for him, though we told them where he was to be found.

A Mr William Wood of Bowden told the same Commissioner:

In a prosecution at Stalybridge not very long ago it was proved that two boys had swept seventy-eight chimneys in three days for the prisoner. When he was called upon for his defence he said to the chairman 'You know my lad sweeps your chimney'; the chairman perhaps did not know it, but it was true.

A London boy chimney-sweep with his brushes

This Mr Wood was so unpopular with local sweeps that they secretly put slates across the top of his chimney, causing smoke to billow out into his living room. His wife nagged him until he reluctantly agreed to allow a boy to climb up their own chimney, when the truth was discovered.

Not only did magistrates pretend not to know that climbing boys were being used. John Mason, Keeper of the Town Hall at Wolverhampton, admitted during the same 1863 enquiry 'I have been six years in this office. The chimneys in the Town Hall have always been swept by boys, with the exception of one chimney which is too small for a boy to get up.'

Sometimes parents lost touch with their children. Mr Henry Beach of Fireball Court, Houndsditch, remembered

> two nice little boys, aged nine and eleven, where I was apprenticed, being sold one Sunday morning for £1.10s. [£1.50p] the two. The sweep would get a good deal of money for them by selling them again, perhaps £5 a piece; as London boys were very valuable in the country, as they are taught so well. The boys were never heard of again. The poor widow of a mother used to come backwards and forwards to our place to enquire about them, but could never hear any tidings [news] of them.

At last Shaftesbury's efforts were rewarded by an Act of Parliament in 1875 which forbade sweeps to follow their trade unless, as suggested by Jonas Hanway a century earlier, they had a licence, which was to be granted every year by the police only if they were satisfied the sweep was not employing climbing boys. This was successful because, at last, people everywhere—even housewives—began to see that it was wrong to use climbing boys. If you want to know more about climbing boys, ask a library for 'Lord Shaftesbury' by J. L. and Barbara Hammond, and read chapter fifteen.

METAL TRADES

Sometimes those who employed young children felt they were doing the kindest thing for them in difficult circumstances. For example John Parslow, a covermaker in an Iron Hollow Ware Foundry at Horsley Fields near Wolverhampton said, in evidence for an 1864 Children's Employment Commission Report:

A toy train made in England in 1840. It was probably painted by a child worker

There are seven lads working under the men in our shop. The eldest is now seventeen. They all came at about ten years of age. I know that five out of the seven were fatherless when they came. Their mothers brought them to us, and asked us to take them, as they were in want of their earnings. They got about 2s. 6d. [12½p] a week when they first began. I know that many children are taken by men in manufactories at an earlier age than would be advantageous to themselves, from feelings of compassion [feeling sorry] for the parents of the boys. Bigger boys could be got for another 6d. [2½p], and be much more useful.

Such children would often be keen to work in order to get food. At another factory near Wolverhampton, the Crown Tube Works, Wednesbury, Edward Hardiman gave evidence:

I am seven years old. I clean tongs. I get 2s. [10p] a week. I can't read. I have been to school. I have no father. My father was killed three years ago. I have two brothers and three sisters. One brother works here; one sister is in service. I come at six, I did not get away till nine last night. I was not tired when I got home.

At a Tin Toy Factory in Wolverhampton, Fanny Boxer said:

I am going eleven. I have worked for about two years. My work is painting little toys. There are five of us at home, besides father and mother. The eldest of us is a boy of sixteen. He works at the pit. Father is a collier, but he cannot work. He has asthma. Mother takes in washing. I get

1s. 9d. [9p] a week. I have got 2s. 6d. [12½p] by working overwork. Just before Christmas I worked to nine o'clock. I then got 2s. 9½d. [14p].

The large size of Victorian families was another reason for sending children out to work. For example Peter Plummer, a staff carrier at Shotley Bridge Iron Company, County Durham, said 'I am gone ten. Father is a puddler. I have seven brothers. I am the eldest child.'

Mr J. E. White, the same Commissioner who had taken evidence about glove and match making, was horrified at the dirt and noise in some metal work shops, and how little people worried about the dangers. He visited a Steel Pen Works at Birmingham, where steel was also rolled for crinolines (wide frames supporting ladies' skirts). He found the cleaning of rollers when in motion made 'a noise so loud as to make one think some accident had happened to the machinery'. There was no provision for washing, except a small bucket of 'very dirty water' which was not used. One boy, Alfred Belus aged eleven, said he 'got the grease off with a rag', which was 'a small dirty piece'. Jack Parden aged eleven found he cut his hands on the metal, but he never stayed away from work, as his mother would not allow it. His eyes had been bad since working in the factory; he had a cough, and he had lost his appetite. His previous job in a button factory had been worse:

> Lost the top of that thumb at buttons, to which work I went when going ten; was putting the buttons under a press for the wench for whom I worked when she let it down. It smashed my thumb, and they cut the end off at the hospital, which I went to for a fortnight, but the nail has grown up again.

Mr J. E. White noticed that Jack stood 'close by a *vitriol* tub. His eyelids are clogged with matter. Is very ragged.' Also in the same workshop were nine children aged twelve or under, including John Caraghan aged nine who carried 'five to seven stone of steel coils from one mill to another all day long'.

11 Domestic Service

There was one sort of employment where about one million women and girls were to be found, more than in any other job. Yet this was not enquired into by Commissioners for official Reports. Perhaps this is because every Member of Parliament had several servants and was therefore confident he knew all about how servants lived. Since he believed he treated his servants decently and provided them with a good home, he did not think of suggesting laws to make life better for them. It is hard to find out about their daily lives, but one interesting picture of child servants is given in a book called 'Lark Rise to Candleford' a novel written by Flora Thompson which is partly the story of her own life. She was born in 1876 and lived in a hamlet in Oxfordshire.

Local girls left school at ten or eleven, helped their mother with younger children for a year, then went as servants in the houses of shopkeepers, teachers or farm bailiffs. They were paid 1s. (5p) a week, given clothes, fed well, and trained alongside the mother to look after her children and do the housework. Of course hours were long and there was little free time. After one year the girl would try to find a place as kitchen maid in a larger house, possibly in some distant town. After years of washing up, peeling vegetables and scrubbing floors, she would hope to become a cook, or she might prefer to start as a housemaid, aiming to be a housekeeper eventually. In these large houses the younger servants were trained, and strictly disciplined, by the older servants. They would seldom meet the owners of the house. Wages varied from £7 a year for a kitchen maid to £50 a year for a cook, in addition to food and bed. The food was

A drawing of 1868 showing a young servant girl and her mistress

usually plentiful. Two or three young servants would probably share one attic bedroom; they would not have a bathroom, but neither would their employers. Each summer they would be allowed two weeks' holiday which they spent at home with their families, bringing generous presents out of their small earnings. Most girls would leave domestic *service* when they married, which most of them managed to do, despite rules about 'not having followers' which may have applied more strictly to the younger teenagers than to older girls. One very strong hold that an employer had over servants was their need for a good reference if they wished to move to another job. A reference was written by an employer saying that the servant was a good worker who could be trusted. Nobody ever asked for a reference certifying that an employer was well behaved, but if a servant girl was refused a good reference she might be in very great difficulties. No doubt few girls would have become domestic servants if there had been as many different jobs to choose from as there are today. But some did find this work had a few good points: there was usually enough to eat and it was physically healthy, despite the long hours, and the skills learnt were very useful when they got married. Mothers who managed to get a place in domestic service for their daughters, instead of factory or field work, felt that they had done well for them and given them as good a start in life as possible.

12 *What did it cost to live?*

If you are interested in working out how you would have managed on the wages mentioned for the various jobs done by children in the nineteenth century, the following typical prices might help you in your calculations. Unlike the present day, prices remained much the same, and did not increase each year as they have done in the second half of the present century.

PRICES

According to the Reports of factory inspectors in 1863, the following were the usual prices in shops in northern manufacturing districts:

bread, 4 lb loaf,	6d. (2½p)
beef and bacon	7d. (3p) a lb
butter	1s. 3d. (6p) a lb
oatmeal varied between	1s. 9d. (9p) and 3s. (15p) for 12 lbs

A detailed personal budget was recorded in the 1867–68 Report on Women and Children in Agriculture, thanks to Mr Henry Kicher, a farm labourer of Aldershot, who remembered details of what he spent for forty years since he first went to work at the age of twelve, even though he was unable to write, and could only read with difficulty. His father brought up a large family on 12s. (60p) a week, so Henry learnt to live economically early in life. His own earnings usually averaged, with overtime, 16s. 10d. (84p) a week. For lodgings, including vegetables, he paid 2s. 6d. (12½p) a week.

His other expenses for the week are shown in the table below:

	s.	d.	(p)
loaves, (each)	0	8	$3\frac{1}{2}$
meat, per lb ($\frac{1}{2}$ kg)	0	8	$3\frac{1}{2}$
tea, for 2 oz (50 gm)	0	6	$2\frac{1}{2}$
sugar, per lb ($\frac{1}{2}$ kg)	0	6	$2\frac{1}{2}$
cheese, per lb ($\frac{1}{2}$ kg)	0	8	$3\frac{1}{2}$
beer, per pint ($\frac{1}{2}$ litre)	0	2	1
tobacco, for 2 oz (50 gm)	0	7	3
candles, for a week	0	4	2

He reckoned that his working clothes for six months cost as shown:

	s.	d.	(p)
trousers	10	0	50
waistcoat	3	0	15
jacket (lasted a year)	10	0	50
boots (lasted 8 months)	12	0	60
one shirt	2	0	10
2 pairs socks	1	2	6
hat	1	0	5
neckcloth	1	0	5
smock	4	0	20

In addition he also bought Sunday clothes, which lasted for two years and cost—coat £1, trousers 12s. (60p), waistcoat 8s. (40p), boots 12s. (60p), hat 5s. (25p). He did not appear to spend any money on holidays, travel, newspapers, books, sweets, postage or entertainment (apart from his beer), but he did spend 1s. 3d. (6p) a month on his 'Club' which probably provided him with simple insurance benefits such as sick pay and burial money, and perhaps also basic medical treatment.

He said 'I think I was always a very careful man. When I lived alone I always earned more than I spent.' When he had a family and 'was only earning 12s. (60p) a week I found I could not live upon my wages, and got into debt, but my debts were all paid off when I worked by the task and at harvest.' Even renting a house could be turned to his advantage by an economical man: If a man pays 2s. (10p) a week for a cottage and garden he can keep a pig and make a considerable sum (probably enough to pay his cottage rent) by his pig; if he is industrious he might make much more.

One of the many disappointments awaiting country families who moved to the towns hoping to find more jobs and better pay, was that rents were higher for cramped accommodation. Those great country blessings, the garden and the pig, were impossible in the crowded insanitary town slums. So the higher town wages did not go much further than the country wage. Perhaps Henry Kicher was fortunate as he lived near to a town and his employer might have been afraid of losing his employees to some kind of work in the town unless he paid them wages rather higher than those usually paid in country districts further away from any town.

13 What did Parliament do?

The various kinds of work done by children, in the potteries, sewing trades, match making, and metal trades were first looked into in the early 1860s by Commissioners who reported to Parliament. All the descriptions have come from their Reports. Soon after the Commissioners made their Reports, Parliament passed a series of Acts to try to make rules for these kinds of work.

THE NEW LAWS

Unfortunately so many Acts were passed, and the instructions given by them were either so vague or so complicated, that often employers took no notice of them, with the excuse that nobody really understood them. A factory inspector, Mr Baker, tried to help his fellow inspectors by writing a book of instructions called 'Factory Acts made Easy'. When a new edition became necessary, after all the new laws were made, it was brought out in 1867 with the not very hopeful title of 'Factory Acts made as Easy as Possible'.

The laws about working conditions were made simpler and sorted out in the 1878 Factory and Workshops Act. A factory was a workplace using mechanical power. If there was no mechanical power it was called a workshop. The 1878 Act made rules about textile factories, other factories, workshops employing women, children and young people, women's workshops, and family workshops. Textile factories had shorter hours than the others, which were limited to $10\frac{1}{2}$ hours to be taken between 6 a.m. and 9 p.m., although some exceptions, even to this, were allowed.

At last Parliament, the employers and people everywhere had

become convinced that the law must be used to protect people at their employment, especially children. From that day to this a multitude of Acts have been passed to regulate hours and conditions, an army of factory inspectors are employed to make sure the Acts are obeyed, the school leaving age has been raised several times, and school inspectors have been given the job of checking truancy and preventing employers taking on young people under the school leaving age for more than a small number of hours a week. At the same time families who find it difficult to manage without children's earnings have been helped by free school dinners, maintenance grants, child benefit and social security payments. The next time you feel inclined to grumble because you cannot leave school yet, think of Joseph Hebergam, Thomas Moorhouse, Harriet Adams or Lizzie Ibbins. How they would envy us!

Things to do

1. Collect personal narratives about their first jobs from elderly relations, friends and neighbours. Ask your family what they know about the first jobs done by their parents and grandparents. You could make a scrapbook, or tape recordings, or write down the stories. (Questions to ask: How old were you when you started? What was the name of the firm? What street was it in? What was your job called? What did you do? When did you start and finish each day? How much time for meals? Hours on Saturdays? Pay? Holidays? Training? Overalls? Safety precautions? Foreman?)
2. Enquire at the Reference Room of your local Public Library for local newspapers from the nineteenth century. You might be shown how to read them on micro-film. Copy out advertisements for jobs for young people, always noting the date, and the name of the newspaper.
3. Ask the Librarian if they have any records of local factories, workshops, mines, farms, and child employees in the nineteenth century. Copy some details about them if you can.
4. Explore the area around your school and home, and see if you can find any buildings with the date, in stone or brick or painted, on the building. Draw or photograph one of each type of building from the period 1830–85.
5. See if you can find a building with the name 'Board School' or 'Workhouse' or 'Infirmary' carved in stone. If you discover one, your local Library might be able to give you more details about its history. What is the building used for now?
6. Find out all you can about life in nineteenth-century workhouses. Why were people so much afraid of being sent to a workhouse?
7. Work out a budget for
   (a) a child worker in the mid-nineteenth century
   (b) the widowed mother of six children (three at work) at the same period

(c) a family with six children at the present day whose father works on a farm (remember child benefits and other financial help).

8. Imagine that you are attending a meeting of a Short-Time Committee to plan for the York Meeting in 1832. Write down the dialogue.

9. Write a poem or an essay describing your feelings as a child worker in either a textile factory, or a coal mine, or in an agricultural gang, or as a climbing boy, or in any other employment, in the nineteenth century.

10. Write an imaginary argument between a poverty-stricken nineteenth-century mother and father, one arguing that the children must go out to work, the other that the family must be split up and go into a workhouse.

11. Make a survey of local part-time employment for young people, with the help of other pupils in your school. Find out hours, pay, conditions, advantages and disadvantages. Ask your School Welfare Officer to tell you about the local council's regulations for young people's employment.

12. Enquire at your local Museum if they have any displays showing daily life or children at work or local industries in the nineteenth century.

13. Keep a time sheet for a week, recording (honestly!) exactly how much time you spend on
(a) school work (b) helping at home (c) a part-time job, if any (d) watching T. V. and listening to records (e) reading (f) walking, sports or games out of school hours (g) a creative hobby (h) eating (i) sleeping. Could you improve the way you divide your time?

Books to Read

Try reading some of the following books. Your local Public Library will stock them, or get them for you.

Tory Radical: the life of Richard Oastler by CECIL DRIVER, New York University Press, 1946.

The Story of Huddersfield by ROY BROOK, MacGibbon & Kee, Ltd., 1968.

Lord Shaftesbury by J. L. and B. HAMMOND, Penguin, 1939.

Shaftesbury by G. F. A. BEST, Mentor Books, 1975.

Michael Armstrong by FRANCES TROLLOPE, H. Bohn, 1844, if obtainable, a novel about factory children.

Mary Barton by MRS. GASKELL, Chapman & Hall, 1848, a novel about Manchester factory workers.

David Copperfield by CHARLES DICKENS, Chapman & Hall, 1862, a novel describing his own work in a factory as a child.

The Water Babies by CHARLES KINGSLEY, 2nd edn., Macmillan, 1871, a novel about a climbing boy.

Lark Rise to Candleford by FLORA THOMPSON, new edn., Oxford University Press, 1979.

Useful Toil edited by JOHN BURNETT, Allen Lane, 1974 (autobiographies of working people from the 1820s to the 1920s).

Ask the Fellows Who Cut the Hay by GEORGE EWART EVANS, Faber, 1972.

A Country Camera 1844–1914 by GORDON WINTER, Penguin, 1973.

Bound to the Soil by BARBARA KERR, J. Baker, 1968.

Rural Life in Wessex 1500–1900 by J. H. BETTEY, Moonraker Press, 1977.

Joseph Arch. The Story of His Life. Told by Himself, Hutchinson, 1898.

Glossary

Act, a law, agreed by Parliament and signed by the King or Queen

agitator, a person who tries to cause trouble and start things happening

almshouses, houses provided, usually by charity, for the old and those in need

apprenticed, in the nineteenth century, children were bound by an agreement to work for an employer for several years for a low wage, in return for being taught to do the work. In many jobs not much skill was needed, and an apprentice was just cheap labour. Sometimes the employer agreed to give board and lodgings

canting hypocrites, insincere people who say a lot of good things but do not really mean what they say

charity, giving kindness, help or money to those who need it

chimneys, vertical brick or stone passages above fireplaces in houses, to let the smoke escape through the roof

civility, politeness

clinkered, protected with strips of metal or metal studs

climbing boys, climbed up chimneys, inside them, to sweep down the soot

clogs, heavy working shoes with wooden soles

coal, fuel dug out of the earth, which used to be burnt in fireplaces in houses. Black, in large lumps or small pieces (nuts) or dust (slack). It makes a lot of black dust, leaves ashes in the grate, and lines the chimney with soot. It was also used to heat the water in steam engines for factories and railways

collier, man who worked in a coal-mine

colliery, a coal-mine

corve, truck in a coal mine

cotton, thread or material made from the cotton plant which grows in hot countries

degrading, shameful

drawers, coal-miners—the men who draw the coal from the ground

enclosures, in the early nineteenth century a lot of common land and land which was owned and farmed jointly by the poorer people was taken over and fenced in by rich landlords, leaving many people without any land of their own to farm

estate, land and houses belonging to one person

factories, buildings with machinery, and mechanical power, where things are made

factory inspector, official paid to inspect factories and check that laws about factory work are being obeyed

fettling, cleaning

gang, group of people often children, employed by a ganger who took them to work at different farms, a few weeks at each farm

getter, man cutting coal at the coal face

headings, coal face, usually underground

hoeing, breaking up the ground between plants, to kill weeds and let in more air and rain water

hovels, small, dirty huts or houses where people lived

hurrier, boy or girl who filled and pushed trucks of coal

Infirmary, hospital

injurious, damaging

jiggerer, boy who turned a potter's wheel

lace, delicate strip of open embroidery made from fine thread and attached to the edge of a collar, garment or handkerchief

lug, an old measure of length

magistrate, unpaid part-time judge in a small local court

manufactories, factories

mill, factory

mine, series of underground passages from which coal is dug out. A colliery

mould runners, boys working for platemakers in the potteries

Nonconformist, Baptist or Congregationalist or Methodist or Presbyterian or Quaker (Christian groups not conforming to the Church of England)

operatives, workers

outrageous, using angry and violent words

overlooker, foreman, man in charge

Overseer of the Poor, man who gave poor relief, collected from rates, to the poor, and had to satisfy the ratepayers that he was not wasting their money

pallid, very pale

parish, village, or small district

Parliament, House of Commons and House of Lords and King or Queen. In Britain the Parliament makes the laws of the country

Parliamentary Commissioner, official employed by Parliament to ask questions and write down the answers, when it wants to find out about something

phosphorus, chemical which glows in the dark, and which was used on matches to make them burn

pick, large tool, with a spike, for breaking up coal

pit, coal-mine

puny, small, weak and thin

questionnaires, a set of questions which are put to a number of different people in order to find out information

Radicals, people in politics who wanted big changes

scandalous, shocking

service, 'service' meant working as a domestic servant

shaft, in a factory, moving iron or steel bar, driving machinery. In a coal-mine, vertical passage, down into the ground

shale, a kind of rock which splits easily into layers

sheathed, protected with some kind of covering

shepherd, man who looks after sheep

silk, thread or material made from a substance produced by silkworms

smock, farm worker's top garment, like a knee length dress with long sleeves, and sometimes with embroidery to gather in the fullness at the shoulders

spinal affection, an injury or disease of the spinal column, the bones which support the back

spindle, machine used for spinning

spinning, making thread from raw wool or cotton

stalwart, strong and healthy

steward, man who looked after a landowner's land and buildings

sweep, man who swept a chimney, using brushes or boys

textile, cloth

Tory, old name for Conservative

trappers, children in coal mines who opened and closed ventilation doors

trucks, carts on wheels for carrying coal

twitching, weeding

ventilation doors, doors which could be opened to let in fresh air

victuals, food

vitriol, acid

weaver, man who weaves cloth, using thread on a loom
Whig, old name for Liberal
witnesses, people who give evidence, and describe things they know
wool, thread or material made from sheep hair
worsted, a fine wool cloth

Index

Acknowledgements

For permission to reproduce photographs we are grateful to the following:

Page:
5 Kirklees Libraries and Arts Division (K.L.A.D.)
8 K.L.A.D.
9 K.L.A.D.
11 British Library (B.L.)
12 K.L.M.S.
15 K.L.M.S.
16 Syndics of the Cambridge University Library
19 Mansell Collection (M.C.)
21 M.C.
26 Courtesy of the Trustees of the British Museum
27 B.L.
29 B.L.
33 M.C.
35 B.L.
38 M.C.
40 B.L.

Page:
41 M.C.
46 Illustrated London News Picture Library (I.L.N.P.L.)
49 Punch
50 University of Reading, Museum of English Rural Life
53 M.C.
57 Council of Dorset Natural History and Archaeological Society, Dorset County Museum, Dorchester
59 I.L.N.P.L.
67 I.L.N.P.L.
73 I.L.N.P.L.
76 M.C.
78 Bethnal Green Museum of Childhood, Crown Copyright
81 M.C.

Cover: Illustrated London News Picture Library and Mansell Collection